Profiles
Stories of Servant Leadership and Inspiration

"Caring for persons, the more able and the less able serving each other, is the rock upon which a good society is built. Whereas, until recently, caring was largely person to person, now most of it is mediated through institutions – often large, complex, powerful, impersonal; not always competent; sometimes corrupt. If a better society is to be built, one that is more just and more loving, one that provides greater creative opportunity for its people, then the most open course is to raise both the capacity to serve and the very performance as servant of existing major institutions by new regenerative forces operating within them." (Robert K. Greenleaf on Servant Leadership)

"I expect to pass through this world but once; any good thing therefore that I can do, or any kindness that I can show to any fellow creature, let me do it now; let me not defer or neglect it, for I shall not pass this way again." (Stephen Grellet)

"It is not possible to be in favor of justice for some people and not be in favor of justice for all people." (Martin Luther King, Jr.)

"Get outside every day. Miracles are waiting everywhere." (Regina Brett)

PROFILES IN KINDNESS

*Stories of Servant Leadership
and Inspiration*

Paul E. Kotz

outskirts
press

Profiles in Kindness
Stories of Servant Leadership and Inspiration
All Rights Reserved.
Copyright © 2020 Paul E. Kotz
v2.0

The opinions expressed in this manuscript are solely the opinions of the author and do not represent the opinions or thoughts of the publisher. The author has represented and warranted full ownership and/or legal right to publish all the materials in this book.

This book may not be reproduced, transmitted, or stored in whole or in part by any means, including graphic, electronic, or mechanical without the express written consent of the publisher except in the case of brief quotations embodied in critical articles and reviews.

Outskirts Press, Inc.
http://www.outskirtspress.com

ISBN: 978-1-9772-2433-0

Cover Photo © 2020 www.pexels.com. All rights reserved - used with permission.

Outskirts Press and the "OP" logo are trademarks belonging to Outskirts Press, Inc.

PRINTED IN THE UNITED STATES OF AMERICA

Preface

This book contains stories of leadership as well as anecdotes of deliberate and unexpected kindness. It is about everyday life and vulnerability.

People often ask me what ethics and true leadership are. To me, ethics is trying to live a good life, but also what actions you take when no one is looking.

This book is also about what I observe, react to, and reflect on—often in complete awe. I also hope this helps you to see that there is much good in the world. We just have to look around us, and we have the power to make positive impactful changes in our world.

Alison McGhee said, "Every moment of every day you can bring people down or you can lift them up—you, one small person—by the energy you project. We choose what we want our lives to mean, and what we want to leave behind. We have the power to write our own stories. Remember that." It is in this spirit, that these stories of servant leadership are shared.

Brené Brown also reminds us, "Vulnerability is the birthplace of innovation, creativity and change."

Dedication

To my daughters Kali and Rebecca, and stepson, Andy. Very proud of you and your own families. Each of them teaches me about ways to lead in this new age and gives me new perspectives on living.

To my friends and family who cajoled me to go into different directions, persuaded me to not settle for the first thing I wrote, and who challenged me to attempt to surpass previous expectations.

To my wife and lifelong companion, Jan Joseph, who brings me joy each day and invites me to be a better human being. She continues to challenge me with her insights and outlook. She also greatly influenced the cover design and put up with and challenged my style choices.

Thanks to my publishing consultant Kirsten Ringer, and my author representative, Dana Nelson, for your guidance, professionalism and patience. Joan Rogers—I appreciate your editing advice and shaping this work to flow. Cindy Slater you have an innate sense for cover design.

For all of my students – Ella Wheeler Wilcox said, "There is no chance, no destiny, no fate, that can hinder or control the firm resolve of a determined soul." Keep your dreams in mind, even if they do not seem immediately obtainable.

And, thank you to the people who helped and guided me, whom I may not have mentioned, but who influenced me to reach for a better way to motivate, inspire, and encourage others.

You know who you are. If not, I will remind you.

Acknowledgments

There are many people to thank. I have been guided by many great mentors in my life. Most are local, and some have graced an epoch of time for a fleeting instant of time and changed my perspective.

Nicholas Lauer, William Monson, Jane Fischer, Linka Holey, Jack McClure, Susan Jarosak, Robert Smith, Tom King, Katherine Johnson, K. David Hirschey, Joanne Provo, Marilyn Corrigan, Tom Ressler, Lauran Hundshamer Rott, Rachel McGee, Carrie Keillor, Holly Tapper, Paula Justich, Dan Dimond, George Diaz, Diana-Christine Teodorescu, Farhiya Farah, Craig Sundberg, Antar Salim, Raj Beekie, Tracy Lysne, Sarah Haugen, John Hughes, Dean J. Seal, Chris Jason, Shannon Tanghe, Carl Wahlstrom, Paul Christensen, Dana Hiller and Jane Littlefield – I appreciate the daily examples you set for me and for others in professionalism and common decency. You also challenge common paradigms and refuse to settle for less.

The Doctorate in Leadership faculty at Saint Mary's which includes Sonia Feder-Lewis, Yvette Pye, Sue Hines, Amanuel Teklemariam, Rustin Wolfe, Roxanne Eubank, Shannon Cisewski, and Burl Haar continue to help me grow leaps and bounds.

Rich Germundsen and his wife Val, Nelson Updaw and his wife Autumn provide support and wisdom in how to live your life, and continue to find meaning to it all.

Mary Catherine Fox, Joe Tadie, Rebecca Hopkins, and Cynthia Ganote – you lead and others follow.

All of you taught me life lessons, and your critical self-awareness of qualities of influence and inspiration we should strive for, and purposefulness on living life, have reshaped and refocused me.

Suzanne Shatila, Bill Johnson, Matt Bluem, Matt Nowakowski, Don Winger, Melanie Torberg, and Sylvester Lamin provide me with daily examples of not taking life too seriously, but also make me cogently aware of what life has to offer outside the walls of the workplace.

To Sandy Peterson, Claudia Osterud, Jill Freund, Theinthein Myint, Betty Benson, Doug Landry, Bob James, Jim Dornbush, and the rest of the reinsurance crew who took me under their wings—a special thanks. Words cannot express how much you prepared me for next chapters in time. Mary Kay Bursaw taught me what is needed to manage in customer service, and steps to being healthy. Karen Malin, Alan Carpenter and Jeff Hotchkiss - thanks for being friends to me in industry. Alan Foley and Joe Casey, you inspired me as managers in your respective fields. Maria Larsen and Jim DuVal – You both helped me to see the beauty of working with our veterans with class and humor.

Mary Henderson, Julie Nelsen, Sarah Rand, Bob Anderson, and Geri Sharpe have made me a better teacher, researcher, and practitioner.

Sara Heinzen, Samantha Zaid, Veronica Murphy, Mary Louise Wise, Signe Nestingen, Andrew John, Ashley Sovereign, Phyllis Solon, Stacy Nall Dean, JJ Kahle, Paul Vetscher, Susan Kreisle, Rod Anderson, Bruce Archibald, Melissa Felland, Ilona Rouda, and Katie Johnson —all of you have given me counsel in approaching difficult situations and given me encouragement and advice.

Pauline Speranza, Shannon Foley Galles, Sean Kennedy, Ray Wallin, Sophie Feal, Marianna Lettieri Christ, Chris Anderson, Kathleen Hanley, Jan Nordstrom, Gina Meacham, Michelle Wessely, Margaret Winter, Rita Wilkins Williams, Renee Wilkins Boatwright, Amy Smith,

Ann Kjorstad, Sue Weberg, Dan Woods, John Laverdure, Brian Parlet, Lisa Murphy, Kevin Chirpich, Steve Werle, Andrea Kehler, Donelle Poling, Chris DeCrans, Randy Nelson, Pam Boston, Rosalba Murray, Donna Poshusta, Carla Kilkelly, Kate Hanson, Mariana Ginder, Brian Gudio, Dave Walczak, Heidi J. Foley, Charlie Gorrill, Jeanne McGuire, Michael Billadeau, Jennifer Coggin, Ray & Carolyn Marshall, Peggy Besaw, Floyd Sellner, Clare Ward Bernhagen, Emily Dapper, Laura Enrione, Janelle Schulenberg, Pat & Anne Williams, Greg Heimel and Katie & Steve Potter —your camaraderie, association, laughter and insights have been a blessing over the years.

My family continues to be one major foundation that sustains my growth. My brothers Tom and Gene, sister Keri and respective family members, and those whom I forget to mention – thanks for being there no matter what. Rich Welshinger, Marie Welshinger Kapur, Judy and Lyle Hayden, and Midge Bolt, Rich Palmer, Mark and Gail Welshinger – thanks for welcoming me to be a part of your families.

Cousins Mary Lofgren, Jeff Kotz and Vicki Tinnell Kotz, Lee Ann and Sandy Sander, Peggy and Mike Meyer, Mary Jo and Mike Hornsby, Kerry Ann Kotz, and all the Kotz/Jobst family cousins-- thanks for helping me to grow up and for serving as a community to change my habits to be a better person. Still working on this, as we speak.

My mom, Rita, and dad, Gene gave me standards to live up to and occasionally break. Later, I often found out that the guidance given by these mentors and sages was right…years later.

And to those who never get mentioned or are overlooked and continue to do the right thing anyway.

Thank you.

Table of Contents

Introduction

Eye-Openers

"Hey, You!" An Eye-Opener 3
The Joy of Impact 5
Joy Is Yours for the Taking 6
We Want to Be Loved 7
Remain Unafraid 7
Time Is Rarely Wasted 9
You Have an Impact 10
You May Need a Push 10
A Day in the Life 10
A Reminder That It Will Be Alright 12
A Young Embrace 13
Are Our Dreams a Blessing to Us? 13
Baby on Board 15
Each Day Could Be Like This 16
Feeling a Presence 17
For a Moment, All Is Right with the World 18
I Can Grab It for You 19
Laughing More 20
Life Saver 21
Maybe I Need an Upgrade 21
Mistaken Identity 22
Pay It Forward Big Time 22
Your Meal Is Free Today 23
Staying Above Ground 24
Tangled Phone Cord 24
The Clapping Vet 25

Unknowingly Change 25
You Got This 26
Your Eyesight Is Still Good 27

New Insights

A New Revelation 31
Acknowledge Our Best Selves 32
Angels of Mercy 32
Being Stoked 32
Believe in Magic 33
Capturing Happiness 33
Coincidence 34
Disappointment 34
Eight Years Turned Sideways 35
Give Yourself Some Credit 35
Guilt and Shame 36
Fortuitous 37
People in Motion 38
Practice May Not Lead to Perfection 39
Self-Doubt 40
Significance 41
The Right Ones Will Always Stay 42
Time Heals 42
Vulnerability and Judgment 43
Wanting to Hide 44
We Have Limitations 45
What Is Your Final Destination? 45
You Are Still Ugly 48
You Have Sugar and Spice 49
A Fail Dream 50
I Have Confidence 51
Being a Dad 52
Harboring Worry 53

Helpless 53
Losing Someone 54

Inspiration

A Short Distance... 57
Elevators... 57
Today Is a Good Day 58
From Rags to Prosperity 58
Hope Is Powerful 59
Is Prayer Useless?... 60
It All Can Happen So Fast 60
Live Life to the Fullest 61
Love Can Overcome Many Things 61
Opening Up a Cold One 61
Being Stressed and Overwhelmed... 63
Break from the Rain 63
Gratitude 64

Everyday Life

Escapee 69
Feeling Pain 70
Hot in the Elevator.. 71
How Lucky 71
I Never Knew I Bounced... 73
No Shame in Spilling a Bucket 73
Invisible Wounds 74
Jackets Multiplying 74
Jazz Hands 76
Just Poking the Bear 76
Just Want Someone to Inspire Me 77
Keep Moving 78
Keeping It in Balance 78
KOTEX Story.. 79

Life Is a Shitstorm 79
Lights Out on the Golden Arches 80
Contrast of Light and Darkness 81
Long-Distance Anniversary 81
Loving People Bears Fruit 82
Maybe I Need an Upgrade 83
Maybe Once Is Enough 84
Moving Through Life 84
My Shift Ends Soon 84
Navigating Life 85
Olu or Oly 86
Ridiculous 86
Sinkhole 87
Sitting at the Pazzaluna Bar 87
Soon I Will Be Able to Hide My Own Easter Eggs 88
She Is the Most Beautiful Woman in the World 89
We Have a Good Story to Tell 90
What Scares You? 91
Would You Fill Out a Survey? 92
#381 93

Leadership

Simple Measures 97
A Wake-Up Call 98
Ask Him About Dogs 99
Balancing Balls 100
Being Too Nice 100
Cognizance of Kindness 101
Day in the Life of a Teacher 103
Don't Wait to Try 104
Doors Opening 104
Doug Landry 104
Expressing Your Essence 105

Feedback	105
Giving Up the Peanut Butter Bar	106
Help Me to Be a Better Man	108
It Won't Be Easy	108
It's a Great Life if You Know When to Weaken	110
Lesson Learned in the Cafeteria	111
National Compliment Day	111
Need Some Socks	112
One Aspect of Ethical Leaders	113
Generosity	114
Please Be Careful	114
Positivity	115
How Do You Want to Spend Your Remaining Days?	116
Remind Us of Our Value	117
See That Light	117
Looking Out for One Another	118
Small Manageable Steps	118
Stuck in the Muck	119
Taking Small Steps to Get Out of a Rut	120
Tap on the Shoulder	121
The Kid and His Shoes	122
Unnecessary Noise	124
Walking With Someone Else's Difficulties	124
Batter's Box	125
Last Advice	125

Introduction

Leadership. You know it when you see it. We also know when it is not present.

Those who make an impact leave a mark on us. Hopefully, it is a positive one. The positive impact is grounded in those who bring us joy and those who inspire us and motivate us. They give us examples of how we can live our own lives and also push us to be better.

You have so much time. When you are young, you may not think about this until you see how this epoch flies by.

There are plenty of people who have opened my eyes. Often it comes unexpectedly. Sometimes, you even have a dream that serves as a reminder of how your life may need to change.

You might feel a presence of someone who guided you once before and now is gone.

You can give back to society. You can bring your community together. You have relevance.

I am not going to tell anyone in this collection of examples of servant leadership, combining unexpected surprises, and lessons learned exactly what to do. *I am going to give you examples* of those who do make an impact, observations of people who can help us to realize our gifts, and those who assist us in consciously or unknowingly changing for the better.

This book is about new insights. Maybe it will be a revelation to acknowledge our better selves. It might be about seeing an angel of mercy, or it could involve believing in a bit of magic. It could involve a story about disappointment and opening new doors.

Another vignette might be about self-doubt, seeing your own significance and recognizing it in others. It might involve wanting to hide, understanding our limitations, laughing in the face of adversity, and developing a new sense of confidence.

Luck has something to do with it. Some of us have been given many gifts. Others have to fight to be relevant. Maybe, like me, you have had a few wake-up calls. Sometimes you may find yourself in a ridiculous moment and realize afterward that how you handled it made you stronger and more resilient, and you learned a few new ideas.

Some say you need to handle world affairs, bring in the big bucks, discover a cure for cancer, champion a cause, or sing on a national network to be exceptional. Do not misinterpret me. These are admirable, and I am in no way discounting them. All of these examples are incredible achievements or other examples of giving back.

But each day, someone is trying to do something simply good for someone else in a simple manner. I am trying to take note of these examples of guiding initiatives, and it helps mold and shape me to be fully aware of the decency that does exist in the US and the world.

We each have a story to tell. So much unnecessary noise is out there each day. Can you find how you can make a unique positive impact? Maybe no one ever told you that you are or that you did.

I ask the question: How do you want to spend your remaining days? Being a more effective leader involves experiencing everyday life and learning from it, being inspired, being kind, developing new insights, having our eyes opened to better ways of handling situations, and then taking action to make a situation, our communities, and the world a place to thrive and empower others.

Eye-Openers

"Hey, You!" An Eye-Opener

Years ago, I was working at a center for the homeless in Kansas City. Each day, we would receive donations from local markets and donors to feed 120+ people in a place called the Family House.

On a beautiful sunny Tuesday morning, a man yelled at me from across the street: "Hey, you!"

It was my turn to wash windows at the family center. I would put the soapy water in the bucket, fill and rinse it out, and use a squeegee to make the windows glisten.

I turned around, and there was this guy waving at me from the dumpster—in plain sight. He had a salt-and-pepper beard. He motioned for me to come over.

I dropped my cleaning supplies and ventured across the street to see the man. "Got the time?" he asked.

He told me his name was Joe.

"Do you smoke?" he asked. I thought of my dad, who on occasion used to put away one to two packs a day of L&M's.

"No. But I used to like to have a puff and blow rings in the air." I thought back to my dad who had an air of confidence when he puffed away, many times driving his Thunderbird, convertible top down, and listening to his '50s and '60s music. In this case, Joe was smoking a Marlboro, with deep puffs, exhaling through his nose with a purpose.

His expression didn't change, but the wrinkles around his eyes exuded wear and tear as well as his ability to smile. He was putting another item in the dumpster. "I have to make sure I get my stuff out of here before they throw me away, too." He laughed.

I realized and fully understood what he was saying. Each Tuesday morning, early, the trash compactor would come and hoist the industrial steel dumpster into the air and empty the garbage and refuse from the past week.

I thought about what we take for granted in our great country, and how this type of life still exists. But to Joe, it was no major problem. He played the cards he was dealt. He went on to also let me know a culinary tip. He mentioned that he could not stand cauliflower.

In addition to cleaning assignments at the shelter, we would venture to the downtown markets to catch some of the produce vendors throwing out strawberries, potatoes, onions, cauliflower, and heads of lettuce with first signs of spoiling.

A Christian brother named Louis explained to us as workers that 10%--that is the top of the crate may be spoiled, but if cleared away, 90% of it is beautiful fruits and vegetables. "We waste a lot of food around here," he told me.

Storeowners and shopkeepers were not always fond of our intercepting the crates before they were tossed in the trash. But many let us know the best times to stop by to pick up the edible food before it made its way there.

Joe continued telling me to avoid eating some of the vegetables they served at the center, because you could get sick, but that they did a good job taking care of the people who needed food and shelter. "I hate cauliflower," he told me. I noticed that in the dumpster, he had a rickety blanket, two small kid-sized chairs, and a makeshift table.

One week, I watched him do it. The restaurant/bar would throw empty bottles and trash and fill the dumpster most of the way. But Joe would time it perfectly, waiting for the trash truck to pick up the refuse, and then he proceeded to put his chairs and table back in for another week's worth of living.

"Want to play some cards?" I was kind of mesmerized by this man, who seemed to just go about his business of living the streets so effortlessly. But this was a home to him. A place of comfort, protection, and possible peril if he forgot to wake up on a Tuesday.

"Yeah, once I had a close call, but people check on me to make sure I get out in time."

He hopped back in, arranged the chairs and table, and then so did I—we played part of a game of cribbage, with pegs of popcorn kernels. "Want a banana?" He pulled out what seemed like a fresh fruit, unpeeled it, and we each had a half.

Here was this guy, who barely had a place to live, sharing what he had with me…his new card-playing buddy.

It was early. Most of my colleagues were still asleep that morning. And I was thinking to myself, *Why am I in a dumpster?*

I eventually returned to my window-cleaning assignment.

Some of you are thinking...*I will never have lunch or coffee with him again.*

But for me, this was a moment of grace in my life. A wake-up call. It was an awakening to another world that I never knew nor previously wanted to see. I thought about what I would do if this were me, and how I would cope. Would I be playing cribbage, drinking to avoid the pain, or maybe dead because I didn't have the stamina or resourcefulness of Joe?

I will never forget the generosity of that man who offered his temporary home, part of his sustenance, a game to play, his creative adaptation to life, and his daily appreciation of the moment.

The Joy of Impact

Anna Taylor said, "Some people arrive and make such a beautiful impact on your life, you can barely remember what life was like without them." Thank you to those who provide that indelible mark.

When someone is in true pain and you can't help them—that is an awful, uncomfortable feeling.

When someone is struggling with addiction, we often want to try to fix it, only to realize that we stand helplessly on the sidelines witnessing a train wreck unfold before our eyes.

Or maybe you notice someone who lacks confidence, but you see the abundance of talent and heart they possess. You let them know in no uncertain terms that they've "got game" or "what it takes" to meet a positive goal. And you reinforce the value of this person.

And then they believe it. And then they act on it. And then they emerge out of a self-imposed cocoon. Or maybe someone else put them in a situation or prison where they never truly realized that light within. But now they realize that their sentence has been served or should not have been served at all.

As we all know, some never emerge out of the darkness.

Other times, you make an impact. And, you smile. They smile. Maybe they laugh, and it is mixed with tears of newly emerging sorrow and joy—where they comprehend that they are growing and changing. And you say to yourself that life is something worth fighting for, something worth celebrating.

Yes. Life is always worth something, but not everyone out there in your midst realizes it—sometimes not at all. Some need clarity to see their value, and others need a gentle nudge.

When we see someone ebullient with joy because they understand their impact, what they can offer, or how they make positive change, in my opinion there is no greater gift we can ask for.

Joy Is Yours for the Taking

Baines said, "Joy is yours for the taking—you just have to let go of your negativity, reach out, and claim it. And if you can make these changes, you'll not only regain your joy, but you'll get to keep it this time."

I know plenty of people with aches, pains, health issues, insurmountable family crises, financial strains, and hardship. I have some of these, too.

I admire those who say despite these issues, "I am going to claim my joy." This is not always easy. Someone is invariably going to take you down, when you may be ascending the joy ladder.

Why should you feel good? Especially when others around you are not feeling the same way, it may seem awkward.

When others see your happiness, they may want to bring you down a few pegs. They may also want to bring you down completely. Ouch. Sadly, it happens.

Find those allies in your life who affirm your goodness. The naysayers will always exist.

Claim the joy. You deserve it, and we deserve the joy you can provide.

We Want to Be Loved

My family was very kind to bring me out to Louisiana Café for a birthday breakfast. Fifty-five and still alive!

I thought back to my thirties. Back then, a friend of mine gave me a card, and on the front, it had a wonderful picture of an attractive man with hands clasped together in prayer, and a caption underneath which read, "Jesus Loves You!"

My friend was beaming ear to ear, as I opened the card. Inside it said, "Everyone else thinks you are an A$$ho!@"

At the time, I unexpectedly fell out of my chair, laughing so hard. In my later years, I am trying not to be the guy on the inside of the card.

Today, the waitress was delivering beverages to our table, and somehow the tray clipped the table, with iced teas, Cokes, and coffees tumbling on the floor and table. No one was hurt in the incident, but a couple of the ceramic mugs were broken.

I was blessed to have family to celebrate with and be inducted as a senior member.

My brother was receiving complimentary caramel rolls, in part due to the cup shrapnel incident, and we ribbed him that the waitress really liked him, and "the next thing you know she will give you her number."

At the other table behind us as we were leaving, a guy handed us a cup handle that had bounced their way and said, "Here. You might want this as a souvenir."

Remain Unafraid

I was thinking about when we are born. We come into the world with two natural qualities. First, we are completely unafraid. We are totally fearless. We have no reason to be afraid because we have had no experiences to make us afraid.

The second natural quality is that we are completely spontaneous. We laugh, cry, sleep, and express ourselves with no thought or concern about whether anybody approves or disapproves.

Well, then what happened? For me, I began to fail. I began to have others question who I am, what I am, how I should act, and slowly but surely I got skeptical and developed some fears.

In my earliest memory (or my mom who reminded me) I bit into an electrical cord requiring eleven stitches in my lower lip.

This may have instilled some fear at age two.

In some ways, I failed at being an older brother—one example is when I was asked to watch out for my little sister, while Mom was making lunch for me and the brothers. My ability to serve as an assistant to my mom failed when my sister hit her head on a coffee table, during my watch.

I also learned at an early age that I might not be the best baseball player, and concurrently, my eyes were going bad, while a ball was hit to me and I lost it in the clouds.

I learned that I had a pretty awesome jump shot but didn't maintain stamina throughout a game.

I found out that a few individuals saw leadership qualities in me at an early age, but I wasn't all that and more.

I found out in grade school that a girl I had a crush on didn't think I was cool enough, and told me not to stare at her. And my confidence diminished.

In high school, I found out that I could get a pink slip for failing a class.

I found out that at the time when I had my first car, a Chevette, that I really sucked at driving a stick shift and gave my brothers and passengers possible neck injuries from not making smooth transitions into the proper gear.

I failed at a first marriage, and this practice round questioned my outlook on relationships, and whether I was capable of another one.

I also learned that a person can do just about anything, but they cannot do everything.

I could continue with a litany of my other shortcomings, but this post would be longer than I-35 going from Minnesota to Texas.

I also thought about what it would be like to return back into that brief moment of being an infant—a baby, where all seems so simple, our fears are minimal, and we are carefree, and completely spontaneous.

But that is just silly. You are a damn adult. Act like it.

Now I see that all of these failures and misfires helped me to see that you can learn from your experiences, hopefully cause minimal damage to yourself and others while growing up, start to see that you have value, and that you have some positive contributions to make today.

So, remain unafraid.

Time Is Rarely Wasted

Recently, I have seen a few people write to me that they wasted their time with some endeavor, employer, or experience. They sometimes feel like this epoch was calamitous and should have been avoided.

There are many times I have been discouraged, only to find that with patience, hard work, and sometimes an opportune break, you will get where you are supposed to be. You are where you are meant to be generally, and comparing yourself with others, or being disappointed with not meeting your goals may be frustrating, but shows you are trying to understand and better yourself. Maybe the time you feel you squandered was necessary to help you find out what you do not want, or helped you change to a new positive direction.

If you keep hitting roadblocks, or falling into potholes, there are always people you can reach out to, who do care about you. Sometimes, people may discourage you, but dust off your shoes, and move your ideas to a new listener or new town.

History shows that plenty of people fail in one or multiple areas of their lives, and somehow that gave them insight for another avenue, where they were better suited to exercise their destined talents—and see their true calling.

You Have an Impact

I was just reflecting on the impact each of you have had on me in my life. A conversation, a post, something that challenged me to think outside the confines of my life as it is, or sharing some story that is just plain hilarious - To me this is what life is about - connecting in some way that lets us know we all have value in our humanity and are a gift. If you find you are not invited to the table, Shirley Chisholm said, "Bring your own folding chair."

You May Need a Push

I heard someone say within earshot that they look in the mirror and they do not like what they see. I heard someone else remark about Facebook, "No one likes my posts" or "I don't get enough likes—everyone hates me."

There is an underpass beneath the Lexington Bridge in Como Park, located in the heart of St. Paul.

There are signs of colorful beauty. There is a tapestry of color combinations that may not be fully explained, but we somehow enjoy them. There is a hint of sunlight, and the trees look alive and thriving. All of us go through tunnels and sometimes we are not sure if there is light on the other side. Imagine the setting. The light I see in this picture is much like all of us.

So much joy is latent inside us. And we have so much abundant radiance that no one has to "like" on a Facebook post to ensure our self-worth.

A Day in the Life

On a Sunday afternoon, I went to Menards to return a water pump that had a three-year warranty on it. The pump somehow gave out in one year. We have this small manmade pond in the backyard where ducks and birds stop off to bathe and vacation. This pump shoots water in a cascading arc within the pond. Beforehand, I tested the extension cords thinking there was a tear somewhere. I tested the outlet to see if it shorted out. All was good electrically. The pump was indeed bad.

I went to the store, picked up the same model, and approached the customer service desk. I started explaining that I didn't have the receipt, and before I could expound on my case further, the woman said, "It has been a long day. You can go, sir, with what you picked out."

"You need anything else from me?"

"No." You could tell she was tired, as she recorded the model number into her computer system.

"Thank you." That was easy. Usually, I need to go through more red tape to make a return, especially without the receipt, but this time I was given a break.

I then headed to a White Castle on Lexington and University on the way back to get two egg and cheese sliders, three mini cinnamon donuts, and a coffee.

The individual taking the order from the electronic box and I couldn't get the order quite right—a combination of the faulty system, and maybe my communication style.

I had made this order before, so I was surprised when I heard, "That will be $9.00."

It usually came out to around $6 and some odd cents.

I got to the window, and the friendly employee again said, "$9.00."

"Are you sure? Prices seem to have gone up." I smiled back.

Then, I remembered $6.43, having placed this order recently. (You might be thinking...I need to upgrade my dining habits, and not go to this establishment so often!)

Without missing a beat, she said, "My bad. I rang the donuts up for a buck each. Should be 3 for $1.49."

Thinking this matter was settled, I gave her $20, and I got $10.57 back. She gave me the coffee and donuts. "I will have your sliders soon," she said and shut the window.

I was thinking...*$20-$6.43 = $13.57*.

She opened the window. "Miss, I think you owe me three bucks,"

I explained.

"No problem. I would call that too, if I was you. I didn't get much sleep last night." She went on, "Let me open the safe. We have been short on $1's." The window was shut again.

I was thinking...*The safe?*

The window opened again. "Sorry it took so long. Here are the sliders, and your $3.00."

She still was smiling. I too smiled, realizing I had a seamless return at Menards in an earlier endeavor. This time the pump worked, and I got to use some basic math skills.

A Reminder That It Will Be Alright

This morning I woke up tired, but something motivated me to shovel the light dusting of snow for a few of my neighbors' walkways. Some were out of town, some asleep, some were busy, and one neighbor brought us cookies the day earlier (so it was time for payback). I also like cool, fresh air (above 20 degrees) and knew I could use a little exercise.

Last night my daughter and son-in-law asked if I wanted to go to a Christmas service, which had a thoughtful and exciting "back to the future" theme. It combined joy, hope, and laughter, and the music from the band was invigorating and even danceable, if you were so motivated.

A man and what appeared to be his young son sat to my left, and we exchanged greetings before the holiday event kicked into full gear. I felt true joy in the moment and was just so happy to be with my adult kids, who were to my right. I was glad they asked me to be there.

There was a point in the service early on where the minister again asked us all to greet people around us, in a very welcoming environment. I extended my hand to the man on my left, and instead of a handshake, he pulled me into a short, encapsulated bear hug, saying, "It is going to be alright. Do not worry."

I was a little stunned but let the comment go, immersing myself into the musical service, thankful for the gifts I have been given.

Afterward, my kids and I picked up a Lotsa Motza pizza and cooked it at their home. Having a salted chocolate truffle before the pie, sharing a few stories, and watching their golden doodle happily play and sit by their feet were such simple comforts and an unexplainable extra magic.

We eventually said our goodbyes, and the young couple went to see *Mule* with Clint Eastwood, at the 10 o'clock show. I in turn jumped in my Jeep and headed home, initially listening to "You Wreck Me" by Tom Petty and the Heartbreakers.

After this rocking driving tune culminated, I switched stations. Billy Joel was crooning "Keeping the Faith." I thought back to the unknown friendly bear-hugging man to my left who told me everything was "going to be alright." I smiled, witnessed some of the holiday lights which break up the darkness, and tears welled up in my eyes. Thank you.

This morning while shoveling, I felt very light on my feet, with little fatigue, and remembered what the man (possibly an angel) said to me earlier. "Do not worry."

Don't you worry, either.

A Young Embrace

On my way home, a school bus in front of me put the stop arm down, and I waited behind the flashing red lights. Two munchkins (three or four years old) emerged from a house running toward the bus.

When the door opened, they bolted toward their older brother and the two wee ones gave him a loving embrace.

It was nice image to see at 2:22 this afternoon, as the stop arm retracted and the blinking red lights dissipated.

Are Our Dreams a Blessing to Us?

Are our dreams a blessing to us? Sometimes I am not so sure. I have plenty, many of which I forget, as soon as I wake up. But my dream last night left me wondering, "What was that all about?!"

PROFILES IN KINDNESS

Last night's slumber involved my being asked to chaperone a family of four teenage boys. Mom and Dad had to go to a function out of town, and asked me to watch their home overnight. The guys were allowed to have a party with ten friends. Somehow, I agreed to do this. I liked this family and the guys, so with enough high school experience, I thought I was up to the task.

"Mr. Kotz! We are so excited you are here," they said as Mom and Dad departed in their car for the airport. "You will have no worries with us," they promised, and we exchanged pleasantries.

All of a sudden they pulled out a Slip-n-Slide, rolled it down the hallway, and turned on the hose, which they attached to the kitchen sink. Their myriad friends came through the garage, each dressed in beach shorts and ready to go. I remarked that it would be better to do this in their back yard, but they insisted it was under control. Sure enough, one of the guys was going so fast that he went through the wall, creating a cutout of his body formed in the plaster.

It all happened so fast. Earlier, the guys were excited to play ping-pong and have a tournament on the second floor of this expansive home. Apparently, it was being used as a trampoline or place to jump from, and another guy fell through the floor, and landed in the living room. One of the guys assured me, "It will be all right, Mr. Kotz."

They had ordered pizza, and before I could react as a good chaperone should, it seemed as if the boys had multiplied from ten to one hundred. The pizza delivery guy kept unloading a hundred pizzas from his modest Geo Metro and said the bill was $1700. The oldest brother said he could cover $30 dollars' worth but asked if he could borrow the remainder!

I somehow collapsed from a heart attack, and one of the guys invited, said, "You guys have an AED machine that could help Mr. K, but is it really necessary, at this time?!"

Somehow, I revived to witness more mayhem.

After all the fun, and a water main break in the kitchen, where kids were floating in the main floor like it was a huge indoor pool, we arranged to have a contractor come in immediately in the middle of the night and fix the cutout in the wall, which had an oatmeal consistency when done, employing thirty or so guys to use an industrial-sized shop vac to clear the water out and add an air freshener to remove the mold scent. I have no idea where the money came from to pay for all of this. We also duct-taped the ping-pong table, and play resumed like nothing had happened.

Mom and Dad returned the next day. The guys were fast asleep from the party mêlée the night before, and Mom said, "I hope our boys treated you well. The house seems to be in great shape. You will have to come back again!" And, then...I woke up.

Was this dream due to something I ate, a little stress, or was there a message here? This is a story I am glad did not become reality.

Baby on Board

At Saint Mary's University, administering, reading, and evaluating students defending comprehensive exams is part of a regular process in our leadership program, where we assess competence. In this process, a student takes a half a month to bring together all that they have learned and address an organizational issue—where there are staff or structural issues, resistance, and internal pressures. A leader, consultant, or new director is needed to put together a sound proposal to address the situation.

The committee then meets with the individual and they defend their position, based on literature/research and tying it in with practice, application, and experience. In this particular situation, we had our candidate, a woman, walk in, and she seemed very pregnant. Not to be too forward, I did not ask. She expressed that she was extremely nervous, feeling a bit tired, but ready to go.

When we had met previously a few months back to prepare her for this part of the journey, I had no idea she was expecting. On this day, in her own admission before the defense began, she told the committee that she was one week away from delivering.

These exams can cause our students some stress, and this

additional one of an expected baby worried me a bit.

After some introductions and helping her to feel at ease, our doctoral candidate beautifully and articulately defended her position to the committee, and she actually rocked this defense in fine fashion.

After deliberation and bringing her back to give the verdict that in no uncertain terms that she had "passed," she looked surprised.

She was elated with tears, and let us know how thankful she was, "People believed in me when I did not believe in myself."

After going through a considerable number of Kleenex, I thought that all of the excitement could possibly induce a live birth in our classroom. I asked her if baby was kicking during this two-hour process, and she said, "I asked her to stay quiet, so Mom could finish business."

I said, "Well, your daughter got to hear you defend a difficult comp exam and hear your joy! Congratulations."

Then, you could see that our expectant mom doctoral candidate was moving uncomfortably, due to the baby giving her a mild kick, and she said, "I think she heard that."

Each Day Could Be Like This

Every Labor Day, I equate this day with school starting. For many years, I began school on September 2nd, the day after this holiday, and also my birthday.

This morning, I walked by the elementary school in our neighborhood with the dog. A grandma, mom, and little girl were waiting for what appeared to be a ride.

Jake presented a greeting, where he sits on his hind legs, and manifests his front paws, waving to his new friend.

"Do you want to pet him?" I asked.

I soon found out that none of the three individuals spoke fluent English, but that did not matter in this instance. The young kid hid behind her grandma but liked what she saw.

The mom pulled out her camera, and looked to me, and I nodded affirmatively. She started taking pictures of him waving to them. Then,

I asked him to "sit" and he dutifully did this, realizing that he had a talent and had their attention.

The girl was beside herself with joy.

Not many things are better than seeing a child in glee.

Only a mile and a half away, there had been a shooting near the fairgrounds. Too often, I see joyous moments like the girl and the dog being counterbalanced by the reality of loss of life, people not treating each other respectfully, a malaise of pessimism, and sometimes people I meet with very little hope.

I then revisit that girl's snapshot of glee at meeting an animal half her size in height and wish each day could be like this.

Feeling a Presence

Do you ever feel a presence near you but don't see anyone around? While it might seem a bit unsettling, don't fear.

Maybe it is comforting to have this manifestation in the vicinity. Discerning that someone is nearby without being able to see them might mean a deceased loved one wants to pay you a visit, if only to say hello and ease your mind. They might want to dispel any fears you might have about their well-being; they want to reassure you and let you know they're okay. Maybe they are present to you for your own reassurance at a particular moment. (James Van Praagh and Doreen Virtue would acknowledge some of these thoughts.)

Yesterday, I felt this happen. We had a doctoral candidate who had been presented with an organizational issue to analyze and in fifteen days had to come up with a plan to make an organization (in this case, a school) a better place. There are so many nuances to each case we give our students, and this is another story in itself, as far as the directions they go and how they analyze and present their defense.

After the student orally defended her exam and some deliberation from the committee, it was determined that she passed. This woman cathartically expressed tears of relief and joy when given word that she met this milestone. In this joy, she mentioned that she had been through a tough recent period, having lost her father, a job change, and the normal stresses we all incur in daily life.

You could tell that she truly missed her dad, and the committee felt her joy, sorrow, and relief in the moment.

It is a gratifying feeling when you see someone triumph. It is also a joyful sensory experience when you see someone unify with a loved one who inspired them.

What was even more meaningful to our student is that she felt her dad's presence in the room. Even more remarkable, I had never met the man, but without any windows open, all of a sudden I felt a breeze, and I think it was her dad letting her—and us—know he was reassuring her, as she expressed how much her dad would be proud of her accomplishment.

Maybe he just showed up unannounced to feel his daughter's joy. Maybe he was hoping for free coffee. But the presence of his reassurance was real, and it is one reason I am a teacher.

I get to see the growth, the determination, the failures, the joy, and the triumphs in people's journeys. In this case, the committee was happy to witness an accomplished woman reunite with her father, too.

Doreen Virtue reinforced this supernatural idea: "Remember that although bodies may pass away, the energy that connects you to a loved one is everlasting and can always be felt when you're open to receiving it."

Moments like these cannot always be fully explained, but this is an enjoyable ride which I wish I could savor a little bit longer.

For a Moment, All Is Right with the World

Yesterday at the veterans' home, one man was prancing around like a reindeer.

There is another individual who always asks everyone where they went to high school. This time I answered a completely different response, and he corrected me and said, "No you didn't. You went to Cretin." It stunned me that he remembered this time, seeing he is in the same conversation loop each week I see him. On the elevators bringing him back, I get the added perk of learning where everyone else went to secondary school, too.

Another volunteer, who is in her late '90s—The Canadian Princess—made sure I knew she had a maple leaf broach on her jacket. It sparkled, like her. Ms. C gives me a coffee crisp cookie and tells me to remain "cheeky." She likes "guys like that." I discovered that being cheeky comes in handy with this cast of characters.

December has been filled with many surprises. The Queen, Ms. G, wanted to do some extra exercise and said that everyone in the room was part of "The Over Thirty Club." Membership is easy. "You just show up." (She is eighty-seven).

Another playful vet told me that one of his sons bought him a humidifier. Also his daughter gifted him with a dehumidifier. So, now he turns both on in his room and "lets them fight it out."

And of course, the guy that always calls me ugly had some new one-liners but keeps repeating that the hospital staff put "tinted windows on my incubator because of the horrific scene."

As I made my last delivery in transport with one particularly cantankerous vet, I noticed the lights twinkle on the miniature tree in the fitness gym, with the star atop that seemed too big for the branches below.

In that moment, it seemed that all was right with the world.

I Can Grab It for You

I was headed to Austin, Texas this morning, and with every weather imaginable under the sun (except sun) at MSP, my flight was delayed and the gate changed, and seats were not assigned as of yet.

I headed to the desk of my new gate and the flight attendant said to herself, "Shoot. I forgot my water!"

I offered, "I can grab it for you. What gate?"

"You don't have to do that."

"No problem. I need the steps." After some hesitation, she said, "Thanks. F2."

I went back to the other gate to retrieve the water, and as her friend at the other gate gave me the bottle, I heard over the intercom...

"In the interest of aviation security, please do not accept any unknown items left unattended from other passengers."

I laughed and then delivered the water to our gate attendant. She gave me two drink tickets and offered me an entree.

I told her about the coincidental message, and she chuckled, saying, "I will trust you." (That I did not tamper with her aqua).

It occurred to me how fiercely independent we become in Western culture. Relying on others is uncomfortable. Even getting a misplaced water bottle for someone comes with an expectation of giving/getting something in return.

But don't get me wrong. I will take the two free drinks and may even share one.

Laughing More

On this day before Thanksgiving, I was bringing John to physical rehab at the veterans' home. He asked me how long I had been here, and I told him four years. All of a sudden, he started laughing hysterically, and his reaction made me smile with him, but I didn't know why.

I told him I have been a volunteer on Wednesday mornings, and he started laughing so loudly, again, that his eyes were watering. I was thinking...*How is this so funny?!*

"Where do you work?" he asked. I told him Saint Mary's in Minneapolis. He again started laughing so hard, I thought he was going to fall out of his wheelchair. I am thinking that this is a great place to work, and why the hilarity filled laugh? I also wished I could tell humorous stories this effortlessly, with no punch line and have people immediately be satisfied with joy.

It seemed that no matter what I said, John would laugh heartily. Eventually, we arrived to rehab and he stopped laughing.

Even though John's reactions didn't quite make sense to me, wouldn't it be refreshing to see us laugh more often in our lives?

EYE-OPENERS

Life Saver

Yesterday evening waiting at baggage claim, door #4 at the Lindbergh Terminal for a ride, there was this lady struggling with her toddler. She was reaching in her diaper bag and pulling her two sizable luggage cases in one fluid motion while pushing a stroller to the curb toward me. She came to a complete stop. Her baby girl was crying looking tired and bothered, probably just coming off a flight like myself.

"Could you use a Life Saver?"

"What?!"

"Would you like a piece of this candy?" I presented the roll.

"My baby can't have that!"

"No. For you."

With Life Savers candy (you may or may not know), what unrolls next in the $.75 tube production package is what you get.

Excitedly, she said, "Oh! Tangerine!" And Mom popped it in her mouth.

I was thinking to myself, *I like that one, too*. But grape was next in the roll.

Her kid was still crying and unsettled, but the tired yet competent mom pulled out her phone, made a call, and then my ride appeared shortly thereafter.

I think I still prefer the tangerine flavor, but grape is a close second.

Maybe I Need an Upgrade

Two years ago on this date, I was coming out of a store, after shopping for an item for the holidays. As I approached my car, I noticed a woman who seemed frustrated and was trying to get into my vehicle with her keys.

I said, "Miss. Can I help you?"

"No. This is my Sonata, and the key doesn't work."

I looked at the license plate to be sure, and said, "Sorry. This one is mine. It is a Dodge. Can I see your vehicle? Maybe we can switch, and I can upgrade?"

We both laughed, and then she pressed the panic button on her key fob to start the horn and found her own car three spots away.

Mistaken Identity

I had a meeting at Cosetta (a local restaurant) this evening. There is an entry check gate to their parking lot. The attendant gave me a ticket to place on my dash and said to me, "Hey boss! There is a spot in front. That guy over there is pulling out."

I said, "No problem. I do not mind the walk. I am used to the auxiliary lot farther away in the back."

The lot attendant continued, "Aren't you Bryan Adams?!"

I almost choked in disbelief. "Yeah. Maybe I am!" as I proceeded to the back lot to park.

As I passed the attendant entering the restaurant, he said to me, somewhat deflated, "I guess you are not. He is much thinner, is better looking and has sharper features."

Pay It Forward Big Time

At church today, we had a delightful nun talk about "paying it forward." She told the story of how excited she was to get a sausage egg McMuffin at a drive thru for $1.19. She told the person whose voice came through the speaker that she also wanted to pay for the person behind her.

The worker said, "Really?"

When the nun reached the window, the drive thru employee told her "That will be $33.33."

The nun now said, "Really?!"

She didn't expect the bill to be so high, but the lady taking orders said, "She has a family. Take a look behind you."

The nun followed through on her commitment to pay for the family behind her in the drive-thru.

On the way home, in all of the excitement, and surprise from the bill, she drove away and forgot about her own sausage egg McMuffin.

Your Meal Is Free Today

After a morning shift at the veterans' home I stopped at a Potbelly sandwich shop in St. Paul for a lunch break. When I walked in, Sam Sham and the Pharaohs were belting out "Wooly Bully" with their music, which was piped in. I put in my order, and the two sandwich artists were bantering back and forth.

One of the guys said to the other, "There's your song, again!"

The other sandwich expert responded, "We hear it every day at 11:04 a.m. Really tired of that song."

After Guy #1 sent my turkey with the works through the toaster oven, paying with Guy #2, and sitting down to enjoy the food creation, an Air Force E-4 in fatigues came in to order her meal.

Trying to stay undetected, I went back up to the register and asked Guy #2 to use my card to pay for her meal, but told him to say, "Your meal is free today!"

He went along with my scheme, and she seemed happy, but surprised.

As she was filling up her beverage from the incredible drink machine, she came back to the register, and said, "Is there some kind of special, or something today?!"

The guy hesitated, looked over at me, and said, "He did it."

Busted.

It reminded me of a friend who taught me in my distant past to knock/ring doorbells for select families, make snow angels, and leave bags of groceries on the steps for people in need that we had purchased earlier. It was a phenomenal experience for me to witness and participate in years ago, so it was time for me to do this once again this fall—this time with a Potbelly sandwich combo.

The E-4 approached me and I said, "Thank you for your service." I also explained that I had just come off the shift with the veterans' home and that "my son has been in for a total of 28+ years, and he should be done by now!"

She laughed, and said "Thank you so much," with an additional spring in her step as she departed. That part of my scheme was my initial intention.

Staying Above Ground

At the veterans' home, I went to pick up Ms. G from her room and bring her to physical therapy. She smiled and seemed ready to leave for her appointment, saying, "You are stuck with me!"

The distinct buildings have different configurations of buttons on each elevator. Ms. G is able to use her walker, and as we descended from the second to the first floor, she asked me what the "-1" button was for. To be frank, I didn't know exactly, but I was told that it was a maintenance floor that neither patients nor volunteers like myself used.

Ms. G asked what floor we were going to, and I again said, "We are headed to the first floor." She looked scared, and said, "Are we going to the -1 floor?!"

"No, we are not. No worries."

With not much confidence in my response, she said, "I want to stay above ground as long as I can." She didn't look like she was kidding.

Tangled Phone Cord

One of my colleagues asked if I could help untangle their phone cord. For some reason, our cords are so long that they could stretch down the hallway and around the corner. So, with time, in essence, they curl up and get a bit out of control for the limited desk space each of us has.

So, I unhooked the cord from the bottom of the phone, and standing on the chair, let it spin, fully extending it until it stopped turning like a tornado funnel cloud in one direction, and then the phone cord was ready for another round of getting tangled once again in daily use.

A person walking by said, "Why do that?! I like mine all tangled up. It resembles my messy life and gives me comfort."

We all seem to have our ways of coping and viewing life.

The Clapping Vet

At the veterans' home in Minneapolis, there is a man named Walt, who on cue, when I am ready to cart him back to his room, starts clapping. Mind you, this guy is ninety-six! He reminds me often that he used to split logs with Abraham Lincoln, and when he tells me this with his disarming enthusiasm, I want to believe him. He makes a slow "choo choo choo" sound, where he breathes in and out. As we get going and the wheels of his chair continue spinning faster, I feel like I am at the back of his train as the caboose. I said, "You are the only vet I know who gives me applause when I push his chair."

He tells me, "At my age, I have to keep moving. And I am somewhat satisfied with your service."

Unknowingly Change

Today, I once again witnessed that people can unknowingly change a challenging day to a good one. I had an advisee demonstrate that perseverance and belief in oneself can outweigh initial judgment. I also noticed that keeping the right attitude in a difficult office circumstance can mitigate problems and make the task at hand much more tolerable and fun.

I found that you can work effectively with someone who complements your own talents, helps you grow as a person, and emphasizes that we are all in this together. We are truly never alone, if we reach out.

I discovered that sometimes you just have to deal with a car that doesn't start in the summer, ask a friend to help you jump it (and who graciously drops what they are doing to help get you on your way) so you can replace a bad battery, and be less late for an appointment.

Also, in picking up a gift for a dear cousin for an upcoming road trip, I was first greeted by a delicious lemonade on ice from an English heroine who paints monarch butterflies on rocks, and her delightful young daughter, a wee three-year-old named Freya, who let me borrow her manatee book, and a few seconds later presented a stuffed manatee for my inspection and delight! I was also schooled on how the chrysalis for a butterfly will attach to the highest point in a structure it can find.

I left with two magically painted rocks and an extra supply of lemonade in a borrowed Harry Potter canister. The same wee young lady put her shoes on and said she would open the door for me, and her mom Michelle had to be proud of the wee young lady because she, along with the rest of these fine people, helped make a challenging day better.

You Got This

A few days back, along the walkway on the southwest side of Lake Como, sunshine cast a new golden hue on a blue rock. I hadn't noticed it before. Words painted on it with white letters, saying "You Got This," glistened in the sun, and there was a little heart on it, too. My dog investigated the little treasure with some interest.

Last night, a plethora of people had stopped to see a bald eagle fly from a high perch in a tree to the other side of the water, where it landed on the shore. As the colors changed to richer palettes and autumn leaves continued to fall, crunching on impact underfoot, it became a scene to behold.

A man with a substantial sized telephoto lens was walking with a purpose to capture pictures of the eagle. He was giving me some of his own play-by-play and showed me some of his best pictures, one of the bird in its best regality.

Plenty of individuals took in the fall evening—some walked briskly, some couples sauntered slowly holding hands, another man limped gingerly with a walker and his daughter close by to assist. There were also a considerable number of cars stopping by the side of the lake where the eagle had been spotted, as word had traveled.

With the sunlight, you could see the golden beak from a distance. The bird decided to effortlessly fly back to this side of the lake, and Mark, the photographer, was ready. He prepared for a great shot of the majestic bird while it perched itself in a nearby tree.

Your Eyesight Is Still Good

After a veteran emerged from his slumber and awoke for the day ahead, the nurse and I got him in his wheelchair, put on the footpads, and she said, "This gentleman will take you down to therapy."

"I don't want to go with him."

"Why not?"

"I want to go with you—the beautiful one."

She blushed, and said, "Keep moving on. You will miss your appointment."

He persisted. "That's okay. I could spend an eternity with you."

As the two of us left (without the bombshell nurse), I said, "At least your eyesight is still very good, indeed."

New Insights

A New Revelation

I had an appointment this morning that was cancelled due to icy conditions. I sat in the café with a coffee, checked some messages, sent regrets to my friend, stood up from my perch in the back of this place, and ended up bonking myself on the head on the lamp overhead.

Yes. I actually hit a low-hanging lamp that had a metal cover on it, and it clanged like a cymbal. Picture those cartoons where the character is seeing stars from a collision. That was me this morning.

Some people think the Kotz kids' heads are so big that they physically can block the sun at certain times of the day. In this instance, when my head hit the light, size didn't matter and the ladies next to me chuckled, continuing their discussion.

Another man asked if I was alright. "That had to hurt," he said as he walked out.

I was glad that my head is a bit hard at this point in my life.

But, as I headed to the car, with my head ringing a bit, I gained a new revelation.

You know how kids operate without much fear, and are little sponges of discovery? They make mistakes but remain joyful and uninhibited from harm.

Think of being two years old. All of a sudden, your child writes on the walls with a crayon you left on an accessible table for tots. Can you really blame the little tyke for drawing on the walls? (Uh...yeah. Maybe.)

But they really don't know any better, and it's unfair to blame them for the impact of their actions. They are doing the best that they can with what they know.

Realizing this may help you give other people the benefit of the doubt and empathize with their situation. Years ago, this was a game-changer for me. I don't get it right every time, but I do see people in a different light.

Hitting my head on the lamp this morning reminded me of this.

Acknowledge Our Best Selves

Someone I admire and respect told me: "You frequently can inspire others with your attention to the small things that go on around you—the goodness you see in each and every person and in the folks you meet—here and there."

"Sometimes when they least deserve it, you still can make an effort to honor them by noticing and acknowledging their best selves."

Angels of Mercy

We had a visiting sister from the UK come to speak to us about inclusivity and realizing our own value. She mentioned earlier in her talk that she might have gained more credibility by wearing a habit while speaking to us, but also acknowledged that wearing her street clothes made her "one with the people."

With a bit of lilt in her voice and a mischievous smile, she revealed that many of the nuns she lives and works with are "angels of mercy on the streets, but devils in their own cloister."

Isn't that true for all of us? We try to do our best in our daily work, but the people that know us best in our own cloisters allow us to vent, laugh, be challenged, be humbled, and ultimately grow from wanted and maybe even unwanted feedback.

Being Stoked

Just saying to all of you, "Be stoked that you have—today."

Somebody just asked me where I want to be in twenty years, and I have some idea, but for all that I know, I could be waving up to all of you from down under, before the twenty-year mark.

I could also still be going strong or be incapacitated. Often we as adults lose some of our curiosity and fearlessness, increasingly getting cautious as life hits us with reality.

A few things I know for sure: I hope I am still laughing and able to give back at that age.

The point is, having a future plan is good, but too many things are happening in "this" moment.

We all have "today."

Believe in Magic

There is nothing wrong with believing in a bit of magic.

Maybe there is no such thing as a fairy godmother turning pumpkins into carriages or mice into horses, but there are unexplainable good things that happen in life. I try to not ask why or how. If I just quietly give thanks and embrace the moment, often the magic continues. Sometimes I celebrate with an extra spring in the step, laugh, or show tears of joy, in the moment. Or, of late I might have a dark chocolate KitKat.

Sometimes we are handed an inexplicable, yet bad episode in our life, and I have had my share. It does happen to good people, you know.

It takes courage, and maybe even some naïveté, to face life's challenges. Magic does happen all the time, and so does the daily negative noise around us.

But can you listen to the songs playing in your heart and head that reinforce the gifts you have to offer others? You have at least one magical gift to give. Maybe it is kindness. Maybe it is courage to face a new day.

Maybe you are taking your first step back into an uncomfortable situation. That takes courage. That also takes kindness—to yourself and to those around you.

I sometimes wish I could snap my fingers and see a person's heartache go away, turn evil into instant good, or see years of their anguish vanish in a heartbeat.

But then, maybe courage and kindness would not be needed for us to magically grow and change into something better.

Capturing Happiness

It is truly up to us, according to Benjamin Franklin:

"The Constitution only gives people the right to pursue happiness.

You have to catch it yourself." (Someone astutely pointed out that happiness was actually referenced in the Declaration of Independence)

Coincidence

"Coincidence is God's way of staying anonymous." I have always liked this idea, yet I am not sure if it is just another reflective quote to consider.

Why is it that when you meet someone, even for a fleeting instant, and find that you and or they needed that time to talk something out, process it, or even laugh among yourselves until your gut hurts?

And, then after that chance meeting, or short period in time, you often just move on and life continues. That person somehow helped you and gave you something wonderful and thoughtful to consider. But for lack of direct contact, we add that distinct memory to our own collective bag of experiences, yet never forget what wisdom they gave us.

Disappointment

"God is just too busy loving us to have any time left for disappointment." (Gregory Boyle, *Tattoos on the Heart*.)

In reflection, I am not saying that people do not let us down, abandon us, or disappoint.

But I do think we have a loving God who sees the light within us. For some of us, it may appear to be a pinhole of light emerging out of the darkness of our souls.

Others have so much abundance of light flowing out of them that you just can't get enough of being in their presence.

If you are really trying, I highly doubt that God or any one of us is disappointed in you. Boundless compassion exists for you. Sometimes you have to cut through the muck and look for that small aperture of light, compassion, and love.

That may be all you need to take another step forward.

Eight Years Turned Sideways

Time flies by so quickly.

I cannot tell you how many decisions, moments, gifts, joy, pain, sorrow, stories, laughter, and life changes happen in only eight years. "8" represents a number that when you turn it on its side also represents infinity. On this day when this anecdote was written, "8" years ago, my oldest daughter graduated from college. I was so proud, and still am.

Being reminded of this made me think about all of us and how much that happens each day of our lives. Each second, minute, hour, transcending into days, weeks and then months eventually correspond to seasons. And, then in the blink of an eye, another year goes by.

Do we see how are lives are moving forward? In eight years, so much has happened to me. To us. To humanity.

I do not take enough time to reflect on the power each of us has to uplift someone, hurt another, change a perspective, cause someone to fall backward, or hopefully assist someone around us to move forward and see that they have abundant potential to make eight years or more worthwhile.

Eight years turned sideways can represent infinity or an eternity. But the reality is that time is flying by, and that gift of life is right in front of our eyes.

Give Yourself Some Credit

I have never thought myself very confident in my abilities. I guess that makes me a bit insecure. Like all of you, I have individual strengths, and for me, a good number of areas where I fall short. There are so many people who have put me back on the path when I got lost or guided me when I needed direction.

Or they have told me where I can have an impact, when I am unsure. I have also seen how we do not give ourselves enough credit for who we are, and we may also feel we do not fully measure up.

God or your Higher Power made you in a way that no one can fully duplicate. Even identical twins differ in ways of approaching life. But that, in its essence, is where beauty lies. You have something to give that someone else has never been able to fully tap. You have the power to share what you have been blessed with and given, with someone who needs your skill set.

Realize that the person in front of you, or beside you, or at your back puts on their pants one leg at a time. (If you don't wear pants, this story may have little meaning for you).

My point is that we are all human beings, all trying to get by with our own bags of phenomenal attributes, some bad memories and experiences, but so much more to offer each other. You may not fully realize your indelible impact on the person whom you just met or who is in your presence right now.

Guilt and Shame

In my past, I met a young man who had much guilt and shame. My understanding of guilt is that you have it for things you have done. Shame is what you have for who you are or what you think you are. When you do not have self-love, you usually have shame.

With my limited understanding of these terms, this young man wanted to meet me as an adult. He was grown up, now with family. He explained that he never really knew how to read but had faked it and was successful in his job, despite the odds against him. He was somewhat ashamed but also a "personality plus" type of guy, who could pour water on you and convince you it was raining.

He seemed to emerge from his past of guilt and shame.

He acknowledged that he seldom revisited these demons, only to find that a major part of this joy was his wife and kids. With them, his shame and guilt seem to diminish with time.

On Sunday, his day off, he and his wife often take the kids to a bookstore. They each get a book of their choice and stay for a few hours, sitting in comfy chairs getting lost in their own stories.

When it is time to leave, they put the books back and on occasion, due to a limited budget, buy one for home.

I said, "That is a good life, my friend."

He said, "I often just listen and hear the sounds of my oldest read the book we just purchased for a page or two, pass it on to the next in the age group and finally pass it on to the youngest who knows a few words, but cannot string the sentences together proficiently, as of yet." The older kids seem to help mentor the younger ones.

"Do you ever just nod off for a nap hearing your kids read, seeing that Sunday is a day of rest?"

He told me, "I try to shut my eyes, but tears well up, anyway." You could sense his pride in his offspring.

I thought to myself that there is nothing better than the sound of your children's voices, making you proud, and witnessing their untapped full potential.

Fortuitous

I went for a walk in North Padre Island to pick up Jan a poppy seed roll at a local hidden gem bakery. A "barefoot parade" to celebrate Mardi Gras was taking place in the area, and many people were either on a float or spectators for the event. Walking along a busy highway on the way back, I saw a car with two interlocking red hearts drawn on the passenger's window. The hazard lights were on and the car appeared to have hit the guard rail. With my second look, I saw that the entire front was completely smashed in and one of the wheels was slowly spinning, with the car partially propped on the rail. I saw a bear of a man walking toward me, and I asked him, "Is everything okay?!" He nodded.

Seeing the signs of marital bliss on the windows, I asked, "Did you just get married?"

"No. It is my daughter's car. She did." After a bit of discussion, he (with some tears and exasperation in his face) assured me that his daughter and new husband were fine, but a "little nicked up." At that moment, I thought of how fortunate the two newlyweds were, and how life is so precious, so finite, and how some of us are felicitous at specific times, and some us are extremely propitious throughout our entire lives.

People in Motion

On a night in class, with MBA's, my students had a major project due. I asked them to turn in their work on my front desk at the break. In face-to-face and blended courses, students meet once or twice a week for 3.5 to 5 hours.

At the break, one student said, "I did not know my project was due today! You never told us!" I took a deep breath.

"My friend...see all of these that have been submitted on my desk?" I pointed to the tall pile. I continued, "You will need to submit what you have by midnight tonight as a PDF or scan it. I am looking forward to reading yours, too."

"I do not have access to a scanner tonight."

At this point, a few other students were giving tips on how he could submit his work, especially in our advanced technological age where there are many viable options. I continue to be in awe of people trying to help others. There are plenty of people who care for one another, and it makes me beam.

With a little more banter, it became clear that he had missed the memo, and it was not finished. It would arrive late, and the student would lose points. (I hoped the added delay would make the work even better.)

Another diligent individual came up at the break, looking worried, and said, "You won't believe this, but I left my project in my other bag at work. My husband is running to get it, and will go to Kinkos and scan it ASAP."

"No problem. It is good to have family and friends," I remarked, a tired smile emerging from my face.

"It truly is," she said, with tears starting to well up in her eyes. "I will send it to your email."

We continued with the night's activities after the break.

I love teaching. The mix of delivering content, group interaction, insights from students and dialogue, and occasional surprises make life worth dealing with the daily mishaps we all encounter and participate in.

NEW INSIGHTS

Before you knew it, we had finished the class for the night, with final presentations next week in this eight-week course. I was excited to see what they would up with, demonstrating their competence and new skills acquired.

A few students discussed some fine-tuning of their plans for the upcoming final. Others wanted to go out for a drink. A couple of students exchanged phone numbers.

Then, the student who had yet to turn in the major project exclaimed on the way out the door, "So...teacher...what are you bringing us for our last class? My other teacher is bringing us all pizza!"

"We will see," I said. Laughing, I couldn't help thinking and then saying, "What are you bringing me?"

"My final presentation, of course!"

My life was complete for this night. The mix of learning, surprises, and even intrigue often left me speechless and grateful at the same time.

Practice May Not Lead to Perfection

On this day, July 22nd, 1926, Babe Ruth caught a baseball dropped from a pursuit airplane at an altitude of 250+ feet. Mind you, the story relates that six balls were dropped before he snatched the 7th one from the sky. Still remarkable! And remember, the mitts didn't have the padding they have today.

He was definitely an example of someone "outstanding in his field."

It made me think of all the friends in my life who come and go and have taught me so much.

Just recently, a brave woman struggling with tumors on her optic nerve kindly decided to paint a rock for my cousin in Clarksville, to take to her because she requested one from Minnesota.

I have another friend with COPD, who continually tries to spread joy by making others laugh, even though she struggles daily with breathing.

I have seen people around me struggle with some very serious debilitating emotional crises but who get up each day, face the music, stumble a few times, completely &*!@ up miserably, recover from the bad episode in their life, and start a new day, trying again.

In 1926, before "The Babe" became a household name, he performed a remarkable feat. (Some of you may argue that it was a slow news day). But, notice that he had to drop a few balls and keep at it, before success landed in his mitt.

When you hit those low points on certain days, don't give up on yourself. You may drop the ball a few times.

Practice may not lead to perfection, but it could lead to a new insight. You can be "outstanding in your field," too.

Self-Doubt

As a life coach, I encounter more issues of people with lack of trust leading to self-doubt. Recently, someone acknowledged that they were told that they "could try trusting people again." I listened.

In context, the person had seen plenty of challenging episodes in their life that left them empty of positive emotions at that moment.

In my life, I have been burned before. Sometimes it has been due to my own decisions. I have also seen enough cases of people reaching their bottom. Some rise and become whole again. But to get out of this abyss, somewhere they had to trust again.

It might have been trying to trust a family member who hurt them.

It might be a significant other where trust got lost somewhere along the line.

It might be trusting yourself to face a fear or something in yourself that you do not like.

It could be an issue at your job, where you have a hard time trusting a coworker.

There are countless other scenarios.

Some of us give up. People can disappoint and do not always look out for our best interests.

Maybe you ask, "Why don't you care?"

Possibly, you swear, and/or say, "I am done" or "Never again!"

Some people hide. Some heal. Some never get to that point. Some of us build a bubble so we cannot get hurt again.

Some of us wear a helmet. (Okay. Very few of us do this).

I have learned over time that trusting that your heart will guide you is very exciting. At one point in the process, I might give up or build a protective bubble. Consider that it doesn't always move along the way we intended, but the mystery that it will eventually work out is comforting and helps prevent incessant worrying, especially in times of trial.

On the way back driving from a grocery run, Jan and I experienced a car which hit a bad patch of ice, spinning out of control. It whipped around so suddenly, and after we hit the brakes, we along with an additional vehicle ended up facing the driver who lost control.

Fortunately, the woman in the car was alright. We were startled, noticing a few other vehicles in the ditch.

After exchanging greetings, with a Minnesota wave, the driver was able to maneuver her car in the right direction and all was well again in this moment.

I thought about how I had to trust that the brakes worked. After the fact, I put trust in the idea that some higher power let us get home safely. I also continue to trust that people are good at heart and some of us just hit an occasional bad patch.

Significance

I met this guy coming out of church in downtown St. Paul.

I asked him, "What is happening in your life?"

He flashed a sign which read "Will Work for Food." It was not the first time this had been used. But it was creative.

His eyebrows raised. "What do you mean?"

"Well. It is cold out. How are you doing today?" I paused. "It is better than yesterday," I added.

"Okay." He smiled with his lips turning upward in a half-smile, revealing no teeth. (I am sure he was a little cautious of me).

"Just got out of the shelter," he mentioned.

"I noticed Sundays it is at 9:00 a.m., right?"

"Yeah. How do you know?"

"I live in St. Paul."

He gave me a nod.

"Take it easy and stay warm, my brother." I gave him a couple bucks.

You may be thinking...I am one of the "last of the big spenders."

"Thanks, man." (Two green pieces of paper we have given value to—transferred to another human being).

I have no idea whether this man was scamming people, had nowhere to go, or needed a temporary boost. At a minimum, something told me he could use an acknowledgment that he was "significant."

Some of you will think I was enabling this guy and creating more problems by giving him attention and cash. I respect that.

But this small transaction of conversation and pittance of cash encouraged me to reflect on our humanity, and that we can never lose sight of how each and every one of us on this Earth is "significant."

The Right Ones Will Always Stay

There are so many people along the way who mold and shape us. There are people who challenge us and make us laugh. And we often lose them due to circumstance.

Appreciation to all of you who stick around.

"People come and go in your life, but the right ones will always stay."

Time Heals

There was a particular day when most of us going outside for an extended period would not be able to move our lips in Minnesota due to below-zero temperatures. Today it is a place where you can throw water in the air and give someone a concussion upon impact, and there is a rumor floating around that a snowman knocked on someone's door to sleep on the couch.

Even last night, with unusual weather not suitable for humans to live in, we still have encampments near downtown, because even though we try as a city to accommodate the homeless, people do not always have a place to go.

Meanwhile, in trying to make sense of people in sad situations, one young boy, Jaden Hayes, who lost both parents at a very young age, tried to turn his own frown upside down. Even though he still had pain, he found his purpose: to make people smile.

When asked by Steve Hartman from *On the Road*, "How do you get from a sad place to a happy place?" with a sagacious look, he responded, "Time."

We can learn something from this young man.

Vulnerability and Judgment

Someone once said to me, "When you make yourself vulnerable, prepare for those who will judge you as weak."

I think there is merit in this statement. But I am at a place in life where others can benefit and possibly learn from what I have to say.

Sharing something difficult with others can be tough, especially when it already hurts us enough to begin with. So, we often just suppress it.

I will never forget when I received "the note" in August of 1992.

I came home from work to find my wife did not want to be married to me anymore, and she had left. Sure, there were signs. So much could be said about what I could have done better and how I could have prevented this. For a long period of time, I soul searched, felt like my heart was torn out, and at times thought I was damaged goods. I loved her very much, and the way I am wired, I tended to be loyal and would try to work things out. I didn't want to fail. But I was no longer considered good enough to foster and maintain a relationship. It takes two to tango, and if one doesn't want to dance, you may be left sitting on the bench.

The good thing for me was that other people were also sitting on the bench and were looking for a life partner. It was unanticipated to meet captivating individuals along the way, and eventually meet someone whom I love and who has helped me see that I am worthy. I have had a very good relationship for over twenty-four years.

The other miraculous thing is that people saw me on the bench, and asked if they could listen, take me to lunch, or just be there. They let me know they cared about my own wellbeing. I am so grateful for this love and guidance.

Today, in this day and age, some people have said to me, "You should not take on others' problems, because your energy gets sucked away, and then you are no good to anyone." And yes, there is truth in this wise advice.

But the fact of the matter is that there were countless people who were there for me when I hit those darkest moments; when I felt that all hope was lost; when I continued to work and walk around—while inside I was numb and in denial.

I woke up this morning, turned on the radio, and was listening to a program discussing mental illness and the trials each of us go through, which prompted some of the reflections I share with you today.

My life is rich. On the flip side, I have seen copious cases (as a teacher) of difficult, sometimes horrible life situations. But we all hit some tough spots, too.

I have learned that one key for all of us is to reach out to others, and to take the leap and call someone when we need to talk.

Also, there are plenty of hotlines, where people will listen to you. You do not have to suffer alone.

Wanting to Hide

Somebody recently asked me, "Do you ever have the feeling that you just want to hide?" The individual had some pretty tough first-world problems to deal with, but they were difficult nonetheless. At times, I have felt that way, too.

But one thing that keeps me going in this complex world is to know that "this moment, too, shall pass." In Chapter 8 of his book *A New Earth*, Eckhart Tolle tells us that all moments are fleeting.

Bad or good, they are here for a second, and then they are gone. (Hopefully, your good or ecstatic moments last much longer.)

Brooke Rothman acknowledges that she tends to say, "This, too, will pass" to herself whenever she finds that she is feeling extraordinarily happy or intensely sad.

She emphasizes, "Not because I don't want to enjoy the good times or ignore the bad times, but because I want to train myself to be unattached to situations. This way I can enjoy the good moments without expectation and remind myself that the bad moments won't last forever."

May you enjoy each moment.

We Have Limitations

In a local café, in the background, I heard "Midnight Train to Georgia." It brought back a recent memory. As many of you know, Gladys Knight and the Pips made this and many other songs famous. A couple years back, I acquired a last-minute ticket at Mystic Lake, and sat close to the singing icon, without the Pips.

She reached the point in her show where she was about to sing a slow, seductive ballad. She offered, "At this time, I normally jump up and lay down on the piano for an added effect."

She then quipped as a seventy year-old, "I am not doing that, no more!" The crowd roared.

There comes a point where you have to give up the keys to the car. Or you are getting to the point where jumping on top of the piano is not your best life choice.

Gladys Knight is aware of her limitations and adapted to what age and life put in front of her. She also did and is still doing it with style, humor, and grace.

What Is Your Final Destination?

I was taking a shuttle from a conference to the small, quaint Santa Fe airport on Sunday morning. I remember when I first arrived at the airport a few days ago asking where the baggage claim was, and they said, "Sir, you just passed it up." It was a small conveyor-belt-driven mechanism. My bag readily appeared along with the other five or six checked bags on my fifty-person flight.

Well, this time routed back to the airport, there was a woman already on the shuttle bus, who explained that she lived in the area. The driver, the woman, and I exchanged morning greetings. The driver told us about the Ortiz Mountain range and the unusual windy climate we had during my four days in the area. I shared that the Drury Hotel, which converted from an antiquated St. Vincent Hospital, had been ingeniously rebuilt and was a newfound delight for travelers.

In the conference sessions, the power was going out intermittently (I believe due to the wind, but others said that the hotel was haunted from years of hospital experiences). It did cross my mind in conference sessions. Occasionally, facilitators would have their presentation displayed on the screen, and "poof," it would suddenly disappear. Then after five or ten minutes, the power would come back on and people would go on functioning as if nothing had happened.

I am a light sleeper, and in the middle of one of the nights, the temperature gauge on the wall brightened up a green color, showed "0" for a few moments, changing from a comfortable 78 degrees. Being from the Twin Cities, I felt at home for a few seconds, but said to myself, "This is Santa Fe, New Mexico. Can this be happening?" It was another power outage in the middle of the night. Within a few minutes, the temp indicator was back to normal.

After thinking about what had happened in the unusual city, I returned to conversation with the woman on the shuttle, who asked me where I was headed. "To Minneapolis, the Twin Cities area, through Denver."

She said, "Me, too!" This is somewhat rare, Santa Fe Municipal being a small hub connecting to larger airports like Denver. She was actually headed to Rochester.

"I am headed to the Mayo Clinic," she said.

The driver chimed in, "The finest."

She proceeded to explain that she had a neurological disorder, which was being treated by Botox injections into her neck, but it just was not working. She was scheduled to have surgery, and I shared that I had previously stayed at the same Kahler Hotel, after teaching in Rochester frequent times, working with the exceptional employees at Mayo from many myriad departments.

"You are in very good hands. The patient comes first." She laughed, saying, "You sound like the right spokesperson for Mayo." I explained I did not work there, but taught many project managers, and MBA candidates.

She had a distressed, worried look on her face.

I ended up going through TSA security, and after about an hour, the lady appeared again, and said, "You just disappeared."

I had gone through security earlier, and she had stayed in the dining area before they check your carryon items.

She explained that she was nervous, but the "waiting and not knowing the outcome is difficult."

It was time to board the plane, and the future Mayo patient was now sitting in the row in front of me.

Another lady next to me was fumbling with her bags and asked if I could put one of her items in the overhead bin. She then explained that she likes reading newspapers, and hardcover books where she can feel the pages. As I began to shut my eyes for a little rest, my new 85+ year old friend let me know how she had somehow survived a massive tree crashing through her New York home. And, miraculously, how she happened to be huddled on one side of the bedroom, while asleep in her chair, when the major part of the trunk came plowing through like a wrecking ball—through her bed. Her husband had passed away soon after, and an ambulance-chaser of sorts appeared to rebuild their home and took her for much of her money.

I said, "You somehow survived all of that, and you're alive to talk about it." I continued, "When someone violates your trust like the ambulance-chaser, do you lose faith in humanity, or do you consider that this was one bad apple in the bunch, and let it go?"

She became animated and said, "I lost hope in humanity. Trusting anyone at that time was not worth it."

During the pause, I thought that sometimes we see life as it truly is and not what we would like it to be.

She concluded, "But, there are too many good people in the world. I eventually healed." And, then I gave her some of my snack box. She wanted the hummus and told me of an Italian recipe made with fried chickpeas.

I thought to myself what Peter O'Toole said to Sophia Loren in *Don Quixote de La Mancha*: "The greatest madness is to see life as it is, and not as it should be." Most people thought Quixote was of unsound mind, eccentric, or just plain naïve. But maybe he was on to something in how we manage our perceptions.

You Are Still Ugly

On Halloween morning at the veterans' home, the therapy room had one guy dutifully working with clay to enhance his motor skills; another lady using the exercise bike who consistently wanted me to be her prom date; and a man who was being elevated from his wheelchair with no leg mobility, to focus on additional arm strength in a machine that looked like a miniature crane.

After transporting a vet to his room, another character who always tells me one-liners and that "I have ruined his day because I am so ugly," asked me if I had a moment.

This time, he was sitting alone in the main lobby facing the courtyard. Leaves were rustling outside, wild turkeys were congregating, and a hint of sunshine was emerging from the clouds.

This time he was serious. I thought he was going to remind me when I told him previously about my mom "taking me into a haunted house and coming out with an application to work there." (But I had used this on him already, and got him to laugh the last time we crossed paths).

His face crinkled in some pain, and he said, "One of the toughest things about being alive is being misunderstood."

Psychologists who deal with this instinct or phenomenon often reiterate: "One of the hardest burdens to bear is being misunderstood by other people. All of us at one point or another experience looking into the eyes of another person and realizing that he or she simply does not see us the way we see ourselves and probably never will."

In first hearing this, it was a little disconcerting to realize that no one can fully understand us.

For that moment in time, I listened, tried to see this man's viewpoint, walk in his shoes, and attempted to understand a little bit more, realizing maybe that is all he needed.

After we were done, he said, "You are still ugly," but this time he flashed a wry smile.

You Have Sugar and Spice

This past week someone shared with me that they had someone in their life that just hates them. You could see the individual was visibly and emotionally shaken and troubled by this. Hate is such a strong word, and the notion of it scares me.

Don't we all want to be liked and loved?

Some say they do not need to be liked, and Machiavellian thought suggests it may be better to be feared than loved.

Both sides of the coin may have merit at times, but I would rather be loved.

In my time on Earth, there are three people that I know of that cannot stand me. (You might say there are many more I do not know of, but try to be easy on me.)

I can see how the pain of rejection, alienation, and the idea that someone dislikes you thoroughly—stings. It's hard when you feel you have done everything you can conceive of that is possible to have someone accept you, and maybe like you, but you finally realize that it is not going to happen.

Life has a funny way of giving us reality checks. The fact of the matter is that not everyone will like you, for a variety of reasons.

But, guess what? Plenty of people do. They think you are the best and you magically connect like sugar and spice, mashed potatoes and gravy, peaches and cream, crimson and clover, or even a hammer and a nail.

So find and hold on to those people who treat you like you are the sugar or spice that makes their day better.

There are so many good things that you possess and may not know you are capable of. Maybe someone just had to give you a push to see it.

Sometimes you just have to trust that you will see goodness, or witness a memorable scene, or offer some positivity to someone who needs it, or laugh with someone until your gut aches, or maybe even admit you are a gift and are here for a reason.

A Fail Dream

As we witness government shutdowns, teacher strikes, Nike shoes that lace up on their own, and some of you who are having unparalleled success—I had a frustrating dream.

In my sleep, I was trying to find a class I was taking as a student. Now, keep in mind, I was taking classes in a high school that I used to teach at and I couldn't find either of the rooms. I walked through miles of corridors before I found a young guy who seemed to work in the building.

"Sure, I can help you," he offered.

I was so relieved. I just needed a new schedule printed out. He proceeded to take me to a room and pulled out very large calipers. There was someone else in the massage chair, and the preceding candidate was yelling "Ow!" They were measuring the size of his head.

I let the young man know, "I only need a schedule with room numbers."

"Everyone has to go through this procedure before we can reissue a new schedule. We try to see if your cerebral cortex is fully developed." The caliper seemed extra-large in scale.

Another teacher at the school popped their head in and offered to take me to my first class, saying, "You don't need that caliper thing." Again, I was excited that I could finally find my room, with someone

I trusted.

He soon disappeared in an endless discussion with another faculty member, and I was stuck in the hallway again, wandering around aimlessly.

Another young lady came up and said to me, "You know, Mr. Kotz, you helped me open my locker when I forgot my combination, but you didn't teach me very much about geometry."

"Can you help me find my first class?" I pleaded.

She also eventually vanished right before my eyes.

This was a total FAIL dream. I am so glad I woke up.

Your bad dreams do not have to be your reality. Thank goodness.

I Have Confidence

On this beautiful summer night, returning from a walk, I saw a man with his young daughter of no more than age four or five, getting her ready to ride her bike for the first time on two wheels.

Dad was gently guiding her in the parking lot of Como Elementary School. Hearing her joy, the lilt in her voice, and excitement at being able to finally ride on her own made me smile. Even my dog was interested and waiting in anticipation.

The dad said, "Now if you're going to do this on your own, you have to have confidence."

"I have confidence, Daddy! I have confidence."

Two of her brothers were looking on skeptically, not too many years older than the young girl.

Dad said with a little trepidation, "Okay. I am going to let you go!"

We heard the young lady exclaim proudly, "I have confidence. I have confidence!"

As we departed, not wanting to disturb this charming scene, there was a loud crash, some shrieks, and tears.

The dog and I turned around and heard the young girl cry out, "I don't have confidence! I don't have confidence."

The dad did his best at assuaging her nerves. And the little girl tried again.

We didn't wait for another impending crash or witness the success of seeing the girl pedal in independent motion into the sunset.

It did make me think how our confidence can be dashed by a failure, but those that keep trying figure out eventually what they are capable of.

Maybe this girl never learns to ride her bike. But I would suspect that she is exclaiming in joy at this very moment with a bloody knee. She has a smile on her face, riding in circles in the parking lot, because her dad believed in her and gave her a nudge of confidence.

Being a Dad

Being a dad is an experience with many facets that I am not sure I can completely articulate. It is a daily mystery. It is joyous. It contains heartache. And it contains change—lots of it, and it happens so fast, right in front of your eyes, while you live life.

At one time, your daughters want you to play dolls with them, read stories at night, go to movies, build a sandbox, help with homework, and push them in swings.

The next thing you know, you are taking them to basketball camp and softball practice, only to find that they truly want to be dancers, and become (along with their team), really awesome at it. You find yourself wearing shirts that say, "Kali's Dad" or "Becca's Danceline Papa" and at this moment you realize they are young women, and "Why am I wearing this shirt?!"

At the same time, you get the added bonus of becoming a stepdad, and serve more as a friend to your son who serves his country in the Air Force, and enjoys devouring a good burger, having a few Grain Belt premiums with you, and laughing about the mistakes and triumphs you each made along the way. And then he has to go on a new mission.

I think that illustrates family life in one way. One day your talented daughters want you to squirt them with the garden hose, and the next they are furtively muttering to their mom about needing a new bra that you're not supposed to know they need. Every day is a new curve of learning. And some days you make a shift from which there is no going back.

Dunne says, "The hardest lesson in all this? That after all the joy, the tears, the achievements, and one day you have to let them go."

All of this change is still fun to watch. But I try not to close my eyes as often, because I just might miss something. Thank you, dads and moms, for making the change happen.

Harboring Worry

Today I prayed to God.

I can't fully explain it, but I am harboring worry.

Unfortunately, my prayers were not answered. Probably because "I" wanted something to happen, and it didn't.

God may not want for you—what you desire to happen.

Maybe in frustration or despair, you pray for what you want, but life is not like this. I need to realize this. Not everyone thinks the same way you do or wants what you want. Sometimes you just have to deal with what is.

I think God has a plan. Maybe I am delusional. Maybe I have a false sense of what God is about. Maybe I am just wrong and am praying about the wrong things. Instead, I pray for what God wants.

God, please help me to see the truth. Help me to let go.

Helpless

Do you ever have those moments where you feel so completely helpless?

Do you have times where you want to have some control over a situation, but you just cannot?

When these difficulties arise, sometimes I just say to myself, "God, I am in your hands. Help me to make prudent decisions, which will provide love, minimize harm, and do the most good for those involved."

Losing Someone

On a beautiful morning, I went across the Lexington Bridge toward the Como Zoo and Conservatory. "Talk to Someone" was the first sign I was able to read. It turned out this day was a commemorative walk for those who have lost a loved one due to suicide. The American Foundation for Suicide Prevention, "Out of the Darkness," sponsored it.

In the backstretch, two ladies were planted in comfortable chairs alongside our path, one with a Leinenkugel and the other sipping a Corona.

They greeted us cheerfully.

"Isn't it a little early for beers?" I quipped. "Are you from Wisconsin? Maybe Milwaukee?"

They laughed. They then explained that they were here for someone they lost.

One lady who commented said, "The past few years, this event has had beautiful weather."

But as she petted her dog with long strokes on his back, she lamented, "Losing my son really hurts."

Her friend took a sip of her Corona and nodded.

I paused, and I assured them that we would be thinking about them today.

This is for all of you who have lost someone in your life. The memories and feelings never truly leave you, but maybe having time with a friend can help ease some of the loss.

Inspiration

A Short Distance

Victor Borge once said, "A smile is the shortest distance between two people." I also think that laughter builds a bridge between two or more people.

It doesn't always work, but it is worth the effort trying to make someone smile and possibly laugh.

Elevators

Elevators usually remain relatively silent with passengers coming and going. This past week, I was scared to go to the Mayo Clinic for some tests. At a local hotel, I descended on the lift from 10th floor to the 5th floor, and a man jumped on board, dragging a machine behind him, and two shopping bags full of clothes and other stuff.

Like a bellhop without the stylish hat, I asked, "What floor, sir?"

"Lobby."

His machine got caught on the crease entering the elevator and fell over, turning sideways. One of the handles on his Talbot's shopping bag broke.

I was in the midst of thinking about further tests, but this man gave me time to pause and talk with a fellow patient probably heading across the street, like me.

"Let me help you with that," I said. It was very heavy.

"What is this thing?" I continued.

"It's my COPD machine, to help me breathe better." I set his machine upright.

"I see."

"Thank you so much. You want one of these shirts?" he kindly offered.

"No charge. Not necessary," I quipped.

He laughed, then threw out the broken bag and stuffed more clothes in the resilient bag with both handles.

The shirt he was going to give me said, "I Am One Lucky Guy."

Maybe I should have taken it.

PROFILES IN KINDNESS

Today Is a Good Day

When you start to complain about all the troubles you have, begin to be thankful for all the troubles you don't have.

"Our lives begin to end the day we become silent about things that matter." (Martin Luther King Jr.)

You will succeed today.

Spend time getting to know someone new in your life.

Decisions should be transparent. You never know who will see the results.

What consumes your mind is what you become.

A moral life will lead to happiness with no regrets.

Spend time to make an important decision in the future.

"A little nonsense now and then is relished by the wisest men." (Willy Wonka)

Your ideas are a good contribution for all of us.

Follow your dreams with energy and determination.

To stay young, never stop playing.

Smile if you made someone else smile today.

I wish you win the Powerball and pay your student loans.

A smile is priceless.

Enjoy your life, because exciting news is coming

You will leave the earth as you came into it.

If you can walk, you can dance.

Hakuna matata (no worries).

He that flies high has a great fall. He that flies low doesn't have far to go.

You will soon travel far from home.

Life is better when other people are sharing with you.

You are loved and appreciated by many.

Eat well. Laugh like crazy.

From Rags to Prosperity

I was inspired with a story of a man named Carl. Mr. Allamby started out working at an auto parts store in East Cleveland, where poverty and government-issued powdered milk, cheese, and food stamps were part of his daily life. He worked on cars after business hours, building rapport with customers at a local shop.

Eventually, he became his own mechanic and ran his own operation. But something in him changed. Later in his life, he went back to get a college degree. He also had to take a biology class. He didn't want to take this course, pursuing a degree in business, but to his surprise, he thoroughly enjoyed the class and was intrigued by how the body works.

Nine years later, he became a medical doctor in residence, and an excellent one at that. There is still time for positive change in all of our lives.

Hope Is Powerful

I know a few people who seem to be living in endless ultimate glee, but most of us struggle with some challenge each and every day.

When it seems like you are at your wits' end (and if you have seen the movie *The Shawshank Redemption*), you might concur with some of these thoughts. But there comes a time for all of us when you make a decision in your own life with a simple choice: "Get busy living or get busy dying."

At times when you hit a major roadblock, or the news you just received seems insurmountable or painful, I still maintain that hope is powerful.

As said in the movie, and by some very wise folks throughout my own life who have cajoled me to make better decisions, "Hope is a good thing. Maybe one of the best things. And no good thing ever dies."

Did you hear that? "No good thing ever dies." Even after the small act or magnanimous gesture that you make, the good still sends endless ebullient positive energy back into the world. Some of you will say this is a naïve approach or perspective.

Yes. You may not get that immediate satisfaction, and you just might get a thank you ...or not.

But if at times you feel like a caged bird that needs to fly, maybe the kindness will let you out of some of your strife or sorrow or get you through a rough patch. Or...maybe you will change someone's life.

Is Prayer Useless?

Some people say they get tired of prayers being sent for others. Some want more action. Someone once said to me, "Prayer is useless." I disagree. Plenty of us fight battles that never get discussed but are still present. I am going to try to make sure my friends are covered with a meditation today. Hope it helps you, whether your struggle is small or immense.

It All Can Happen So Fast

For me, a routine physical turned out to be a signal for further tests, and before I knew it, I had a diagnosis, where the news from the doctor was: "I have some bad news for you."

My heart began to sink.

For some of us, sometimes you know it is coming. Other times in our lives, it is like you feel the rumbling of thunder in the distance, and suddenly before you know it, lightning strikes and rain descends on you.

And, sometimes you are drenched—maybe even deluged—by bad news.

Possibly, you find shelter before it actually hits your own life like a torrential storm. Take advantage of these moments of reprieve and enjoy your time of solace or ebullient joy you have at this moment!

Well, I received some news that wasn't as favorable as hoped. But it is going to be okay.

Maybe you have had a day like that. Or a week? Or a month?

Hopefully, that small rut or major crisis you are in eventually becomes an opportunity to refocus. Open your eyes to your own value and clarity for your next positive yet meaningfully impactful move forward.

INSPIRATION

Live Life to the Fullest

There is no doubt that each of us hits low points in our lives. You might have it happen to you when you least expect it. Some people hit bottom more than others. Some need others to tell them they are at the bottom of a trough and how to get out. Others live life to the fullest, and it doesn't turn out to be a party. But being in the trough once in a while may be a part of life you need to go through.

Living life to the fullest could mean laughing when you have that time with friends and/or family. It may mean grieving with someone who lost a loved one. It might involve wrangling in debate with a colleague who wants to see your motivation for why you take particular actions each day and learning a thing or two from the dialogue.

It could be the exhilaration of seeing a new baby smiling; someone getting their first job and you drove them to the interview; witnessing your friend's happiness at receiving an award for a job well done; going to a movie with your kids; seeing the first snow fall each season; feeling the glistening sunshine hitting your face; sensing the moment when you finally stand up to a bully with grace and dignity; fighting for justice and realizing you made the right decision; or when you simply keep your eyes and ears open to see the daily good in front of you. It is there.

Love Can Overcome Many Things

Love can overcome many things. There is good in each and every person, but we also have to cultivate it. Thank you to those who have helped me along the way. Yes, there is sorrow in our world. But there are also joy, laughter, and time for growth and compassion.

Opening Up a Cold One

Early this afternoon, I just finished a volunteer rehab transport stint with our veterans in Minneapolis. On occasion, I go back over the bridge to St. Paul after my shift and head to Potbelly's for a sandwich.

In front of me, I noticed three servicemen in fatigues, discussing what they were getting for lunch. Meanwhile, the sandwiches entered into a conveyor belt, where they were toasted. Another individual behind the counter completed the sandwich with selected toppings.

My order came up. I said to the friendly worker, out of earshot of the guys in front of me, "Please cover the three men in front of me. Just make sure they don't order a steak. Don't tell them."

At the same time, I was thinking of our son Andy, and all who serve us in the different branches of the military.

She laughed and nodded.

When the officer in charge got to the register, he pulled out his wallet.

"No charge today. It has been covered."

"What! No way?!"

The next guy in line pulled out his wallet. "Same issue." She smiled. "No charge."

"I should have ordered a shake, too," he chuckled.

The third guy reached for his wallet. "Oh, shoot. I left it in the car."

"No problem. Your meal is covered today."

"Seriously?"

I got to the register and settled the bill. I sat down, and in the middle of my lunch, someone "outted" me.

I went to see two of the three guys at their table. The other headed back to the base. I thanked them for their continued service. They happened to be Air Force personnel.

I explained that Andy had been in the Air Force for 28+ years. We talked about what he did, his rank, and where he had been.

"Isn't there a law against you guys serving more than twenty years?!" They were patient with me and laughed.

I continued, "You guys might appreciate this. My son sends us pictures of the different beers and ales he tastes and tests from each area where he has been stationed." I showed them a picture of Andy holding a delicious pale ale inside a grocery store in Dayton, Ohio.

"They allow you to open a cold one IN the grocery store."

We laughed, and they explained how they work hand in hand

with the army, and some of their special missions.

"We should have that policy in Minnesota," one of the guys quipped, as I left.

Being Stressed and Overwhelmed

"Many of us feel stressed and get overwhelmed, not because we've taken on too much. It's because we've taken on too little of what really strengthens us." (Marcus Buckingham)

Break from the Rain

It had already rained last night, but as we started out, it was a still, calm and cool morning. Within a few minutes, it started to sprinkle water lightly from the sky.

We went up the hill toward Hamm Falls, and with an eager dog, who was joyous to be out strutting his stuff in some tolerable weather, we found an ash tree for shelter to plan the rest of our walk.

You could hear the Hmong Festival in the distance and smell the delicious cooking. And then the rain came in a deluge.

I thought to myself how refreshing it was, and yet, at the same time, how drenched the little mammal and I had become.

Along the way, there are these small patches of dry land that we would occasionally stop at and get a reprieve from the storm.

I thought about people who say things like "I never get a break in life," or "If only I could get away from this bad situation."

I smiled atop a hill that overlooks Lake Como and Nagasaki Road, as the dog and I reached another oasis of dryness, and we each got a brief break from the rain.

I felt gratitude in a moment for still being able to walk with another small life, hear people laugh and celebrate, seeing a guy named Papa Pez on a bike, runners pushing themselves to faster paces, an occasional turtle scurrying on the path, seeing my friend who carries his golf club for protection (maybe he works on his short game, too), lovers holding hands, and seeing us all get a reprieve from the intense heat under a shade tree.

Gratitude

I appreciate having endurance and that I have two legs that function fairly well to walk the dog around the lake. I appreciate the little guy's underbite. It makes him unique.

Hearing the red-winged blackbird chirp on the north side of the lake is always a welcome sound and sight.

Occasionally, a sole turtle or family will cross the path, and many step aside to watch in awe their parade-like progression to the other side of the path.

I admire people who proudly wear patriotic colors for Independence Day. Thanks to all who served and serve our country.

I am grateful when people say, "Good Morning!" Because, at this moment, it is good.

I smiled as I saw tight-knit Hmong families getting ready for the upcoming festival today in St. Paul.

I am thankful I have a brother who will visit Fort Snelling with me to see lost family members. We visited our dad and then decided to walk together to another family site. I appreciated that ten-minute walk to connect with my brother.

I am happy I can share news with my sister regarding an upcoming concert and reminisce about times gone by.

I enjoyed seeing my other brother at Mickey's Diner on Seventh and having some laughs about the past and present.

I appreciate having a wife and friend who likes to spend some time together, but also gives me room to breathe. And who likes to laugh.

I appreciate seeing my injured mom functioning in her protective boot, even though she has a few more weeks left to spend in this contraption.

I am thankful that I could listen to an old colleague broadcast the Miesville Mudhens on the radio today.

I was in awe of a neighbor backing in a car and trailer into his driveway. (Why is going forward easier than going backward?)

This past week, I was again thankful for the men and women at

INSPIRATION

the veterans' home, who inspire me with their wisdom, sometimes caustic humor, teasing, and resilient outlook on life.

I am happy that I can drive to a Dunkin' Donuts and get my wife an old-fashioned cake donut. Coincidentally, I can enjoy a double-chocolate cake donut, with a delicious dark roast.

I get ecstatic when my mom sends me a message, wanting me to call her and talk more often.

I am at a joyful loss for words that I had the opportunity to visit with cousins, some for the first time, who were welcoming and taught me some new life lessons.

I feel an inexplicable awe to meet with my daughters (whom I once considered my baby girls), who now are adults with things to say and characters being built.

I am bemused that I can see former students and current ones grow into their own phenomenal selves.

Although we have some pretty mystifying and horrific things happen in our world, I am blessed that there will be at least one good thing each day I can hold on to.

Once in a while someone gives me a donation for my book, and says, "Thank you." Plus they give me a tip, and advise me to "go buy someone a cup of coffee and pay it forward."

I am grateful to people who live lives of service, are still smiling about it, and are not too much the worse for wear.

I get a kick out of veterans who give me a lot of %&*!, but I know deep down that they appreciate me pushing their chairs to and from physical therapy.

I am grateful that when I wake up in pain, that after I am upright, I can still move and contribute.

I am joyful that I can still laugh to the point of making myself cry. That is an unannounced, yet wondrous feeling.

Gratitude.

Everyday Life

Escapee

In the news in the heart of winter, we have had a few incidents of people making up stories to get attention; in other cases we have high-powered people deliberating whether walls are necessary; record snowfalls in many areas of the country; uplifting stories of kids doing good things in the world (my nephew just made a potato battery); and witnessing parents who are struggling to meet their obligations—somehow melding work, life, and family in a medley of making it all work out.

Meanwhile, in St. Paul, I was just finishing my morning ritual of shoveling (at least it seems like a ritual), and my neighbor alerted me, "Your poodle escaped." Another first-world problem to face.

Being a little oblivious, into my craft of heaving snow, and not seeing what he was trying to tell me, (the snow mounds are approaching the height of the high Sierras), I said, "Huh?"

My neighbor was kind enough to let me know, "Your dog is over here. What is his name again?"

"Jake."

He checked his name plate. "It is Jake, alright."

"Thanks. I didn't know what you were talking about. He looks like a poodle, but he is a Bichon Shitzu mix." I was puzzled.

I walked across the street. "Yeah. That's him," I lamented.

My wife and I always wondered how he escaped. This time he leapt over the back chain-link fence for his adventure, and ended up across the street.

"Thanks, man."

"Come here!" He bolted toward me, but just when I was about to catch him he made a U-turn and ran through a few neighbors' yards, avoided a delivery truck, and ventured through an alley.

Calling him wasn't working. So, I went through a few neighbors' back yards, using *Forensic Files*-like skills. Joe Kenda might have been proud of my ability to follow his tracks, and lo and behold, there was "Mr. Escape Artist" sitting in a snow bank. He looked kind of sheepish, and I told him in a scornful tone, "Mama is not going to be happy."

Incidentally, "If mama is not happy, NOBODY is happy." Thankfully, I handled this one on my own, with my neighbor's astute assistance.

I grabbed him, thanked my neighbor, and headed inside with the escapee. I guess I couldn't blame him for making a run for it in this season.

Feeling Pain

Do you ever feel pain?

I have a friend going through cancer. The process she is going through is hard to believe as she confronts the struggle with chemo, losing her energy and her beautiful hair, and feelings of the unknown. It is painful to see her battle.

I have students who wrestle with their own strengths and inadequacies, but who really want to get to fully understanding their next steps. Challenging yourself can be difficult, rewarding, and often painful.

I have friends who have lost loved ones, not always fully comprehending why. Some have lost family because of natural causes, but it still hurts. Loss is painful.

Last week, I saw a homeless man at 94th and Dale yelling, "You have no idea what it means to be me!" with a few expletives intermixed. That was painful, to see him truly upset.

I see people I care for losing their memory and forgetting that we just went to the doctor together or had lunch. They smile and recognize certain aspects, but you feel like you are not connecting with them. That is painful.

I still see people not accepting others because they are different or chose a path not quite like their own. When you have been shunned or rejected, I have seen and heard countless stories about those rifts, and that is painful.

In all of these instances, you need courage. You need to be brave. You have to realize that sometimes you are feeling alone, and often

EVERYDAY LIFE

you have to confront problems in isolation.

Other times you will feel surrounded by love and encouragement.

The world keeps spinning. God loves you. Many people do, too! It is often painful to see what people go through. We can make it better by not just offering empathy or sympathy, but by exuding compassion to walk with someone in their own journey.

Hot in the Elevator

So, I was pushing a few vets back and forth to physical therapy. In one of the buildings was an attractive young lady cleaning and washing the inside of one of the elevators. We exchanged greetings. The funny thing is that for over an hour, I would get on this same lift, and there she was. I traversed to the other building to get another vet and would come back and there she was again, working on that same elevator.

I remarked, "It is getting warm in this building."

She said, "Yeah. But it really gets hot when you get on the elevator with me." And then she laughed, with an engaging smile.

My radar is not on for this type of thing. I have a wife, who is more woman than I can handle at the moment. I also might get a severe talking-to or worse, if I responded to this young siren with a flirtatious comeback—and she found out.

I told Jan about this random event later that day, and she said, "She was flirting with you. And you are an attractive ...OLDER man."

OLDER man! I felt so ancient that Thomas Jefferson still owes me a quarter. Or possibly, George Washington Carver sat behind me in third grade! OLDER?!

How Lucky

Friday, while driving home, I was reflecting on how "lucky" I am.

This weekend I was able to get an ice-cold water outside the fairgrounds for $1. That morning, my dog jumped on my lap to give me a smooch on the cheek, after taking a much-needed walk. Jan took me to Kyoto Sushi earlier in the day, and we had some wonderful food and laughs. "Sexy Girl" and "Slammin' Salmon" Maki rolls are truly delicious.

Then, that same night, I was stopped by the police on Dale Street.

After the standard, "Good evening. Can I see your license? Do you realize how fast you were going?" questions from St. Paul's finest, the officer proceeded to tell me I was going 37 mph in a 30-mph zone. Busted. I had no argument in me.

"Where are you coming from?" he politely inquired.

"I was playing tennis," I said. I had a 5:30 match in the West Metro area that went a bit over two hours. It was after 9 p.m. when I was stopped.

"Tennis? At this hour?!"

"Yes, sir. A USTA match, in Minnetonka."

"I see you live a few blocks from here," he said as he examined my license and flashed a light at me and my back seat. "I grew up in this neighborhood," the policeman proudly stated.

"Yes, it has been over twenty-three years. Love St. Paul," I chimed in.

We had a few laughs about the area and all of the new Lime Bikes parked everywhere, and how they seemed to multiply.

"Paul. Have you been drinking tonight?"

"No, sir." (It was true. Although I was in some pain—my left foot hurt, my knee was bruised, and, well...I qualify at this writing for a 55+ senior menu at some establishments. Things generally ache. I wished I had something to numb the pain. Just sayin'.)

"Well, we are checking to make sure people are not drinking, driving, and under the influence." Again, I was thinking that I could have used a nice cold pale ale at this time.

"No. Not tonight, Officer."

I mentioned that while driving north on Dale I noticed his car, but then realized I was slightly over the speed limit, and sure enough—I saw the lights flash.

"I am going to let you off tonight."

He continued. "Tennis, huh?" He flashed his light in my back seat again. My bag with all my gear was displayed.

Life hasn't always been this way or proceeded relatively smoothly. But for this brief patch in time, I am lucky.

I Never Knew I Bounced

On an overcast morning, I went for a walk in Seattle. We were out here to see two grandkids for graduation—one from high school, the other from college. On my way back to where we were staying, I got hit by a green pickup truck.

Luckily the truck was idle before it proceeded on to the main highway and clipped me from the side. I did a little jump, bounced and rolled over part of the hood, and landed on my feet. The driver rolled his window down, and said, "Are you alright?"

I said, "I am not sure, yet...."

He checked again. "Are you sure you're okay?"

I asked him if he had insurance, just in case. He said, "I do not. I am glad you're okay." Then, he drove off in a hurry.

I never knew I bounced.

No Shame in Spilling a Bucket

My wife told me that I needed to get a haircut, so I ventured over to Great Clips, put my name on the list and waited for a stylist. I was just sitting down, and one of the workers dropped this very large bucket of combs, clips, and even barrettes all over the floor.

Myriad colors of all sized shapes of combs came tumbling, bouncing all over the place. It was early in the morning. A few people were checking their phones, one guy looked up, and resumed scrolling his device.

The lady was struggling. I thought I would leave her be. But you really had to be there to see the abundance of combs strewn all over. I walked over to lend a hand.

She got most of them, scurrying around nervously. I went over to the site of the spill, got down on my knees and picked up a few handfuls. "I am so embarrassed," she shared.

I empathized: "No worries. I spill juice, coffee, and trip over untied shoelaces all the time."

"I appreciate it," she said.

The other stylists were busy snipping, yelling out, "Should I use a clipper #4 or #6?"

"Oh. You want the scissors instead? No problem."

With the exception of a few combs that took an additional bounce, the hundreds of combs and clips were restored back to the pail.

I mentioned this incident to my wife, who was impressed with my haircut. I was glad, since she gave me the mandate to get this trim.

She said, "There should be no shame in spilling a bucket of combs."

I agreed. We all make mistakes.

I also thought about how our lives often experience a temporary disruption or are in disarray like these combs strewn around. But after you clean up your own mess, put things back in your own bucket, maybe get some help from others, things go back to normal for a while, before your next challenge appears. Maybe you spill your own bucket. The challenge or predicament may be small, medium, or mammoth-sized in proportion.

The key element I paused to dwell on is that it gets better. You just keep trying and allowing yourself to witness your ability to manage everyday life.

Invisible Wounds

I often take for granted what it is like to enjoy each day. I have learned that in working with veterans, previous experiences and situations can make a day where the sun is shining, people are laughing, and birds are singing seem hard to face. Especially when you suffer from PTSD. Thanks to all of the vets who put their life on hold for us. We appreciate your service, and we thank you.

Jackets Multiplying

I ordered a couple of jackets online at discounted prices through a popular merchandiser. Within four days, the two jackets arrived.

EVERYDAY LIFE

After I opened the first package, another package appeared with the same two types of jackets. And, then the next day, I received two more packages, of the same two jackets. They were multiplying.

My wife asked me, "What are all of these for?" I thought that maybe when I put in the credit information to order, I might have hit the button too many times.

To complicate matters, the sizes were too small. A "Large" is a bit like a "Medium" in fit for these brands.

So, now instead of two jackets that do not fit, I have eight!

I called the online store, and they said, "You would be better off taking them directly to the local store for a return."

The online rep and I were both laughing on the phone, as I shared that I felt like I hit the jackpot, having been billed for one order, and receiving four sets.

It is like winning a vacation that didn't quite fit your expectations.

So, this evening I went to the customer service area at the local outlet and explained what happened. Both of the sales professionals gave me quizzical looks, and one of the ladies started smiling. "Most of our customers are dissatisfied, don't have a receipt, got the wrong size, try to return things that are a few years old, or don't like what they purchased."

"Seriously, you got eight jackets?" the smiling one said.

"Yes," I said, as I again focused on the pile I had placed on the counter.

They credited me back for the initial two jackets that I did in fact purchase.

Meanwhile they called in "Nick," the manager who handles unusual issues.

After I explained what happened again, he said, "Oooooh, these are my size. Heh. Heh. I like this one jacket you brought back to us." He continued, "No. We will sell them back to consumers. You know.... you could have kept these, since you were not billed for them."

"Yes, but they would be a little tight. Not enough closet space

75

PROFILES IN KINDNESS

either, and they do not belong to me. They only billed me for one order," I offered.

After Nick called the shipping department out East, he told me, "Yes, it was a mistake. We will give you fifty bucks back, for being honest."

I said, "Thanks, Nick—I suppose you could have four jackets of the same kind in your own wardrobe. Rotate them for the rest of your life."

As I left, he was still swooning over the style. "Ooooh, I like this one."

Jazz Hands

I ordered a shirt online but found I could return it at the Mall of America, in a newly created store onsite. The shirt was so tight that you could shake my hand and check my blood pressure. Guys at my age cannot wear this tight clothing without getting arrested.

I get lost in places like the Mall—especially around the holidays, and need a destination and purpose to keep me focused. When you look at the marquees in these mega structures to find places—you know, where it shows, "You are here"—there is now a touch screen that gives you personalized walking directions to make your experience less hassle. Snap. Love it.

In the distance, kids were singing, enormous holiday trees were lit up, and people around me seemed a bit gleeful. Another snap.

I ventured toward the kids singing songs and paused to hear the three selections. They ended the last number with some deliberate displays of jazz hands while the crowd clapped, and I smiled.

Just Poking the Bear

As I was winding my way toward the north gate of the state fair with myriad swarms of people, two little kids in front of me were getting a little restless, pushing each other and one hitting the other on the head.

It appeared that mom was trying to manage a family of three kids, and dad, who was a big guy, was leading the pack.

The pushing, pinching and ear-twapping continued. All of a sudden, Mom said to the two little ruffians, "You know," (pointing and referring to the Papa), "You are just poking the bear, who brought you here, if ya know what I am saying. Knock it off."

The two little guys looked at each other and became refreshingly quiet.

Just Want Someone to Inspire Me

Yesterday, I bought lunch at one of my "go-to" places and the woman behind the counter dished out the special for the day. She smiled and mentioned, as she scooped chicken and potatoes out of the pan, that she still had the short letter I gave her displayed on her fridge.

At the time (four months earlier), she seemed to be struggling and asked me, "Do you ever get tired of the daily grind of life? What do you do when you need a change?"

Her usual optimism, concern for others, and superior customer service hit a roadblock that day, due to some problem with supply ordering and an employee conflict.

So, in a short note, the next morning in search of a coffee, I affirmed these three qualities that I admired and gave her a note that said in no uncertain terms that she had value to all of us, and we were grateful to have her in our midst at breakfast and lunch opportunities.

Mark Twain said, "I can live for two months on a good compliment."

It sure doesn't hurt to know you do something right each day.

Ralph Waldo Emerson said, "Our chief desire is someone who will inspire us to be what we could be."

So if Emerson is right, we just want at least one person who can see our potential or existing gifts.

There are so many people who do not see the joy and goodness they bring to the table of life every day.

An affirmation may be all they need to get back on track.

Keep Moving

Someone asked me seriously, "Don't you ever get depressed?"

I said, "Yes! But I keep moving, so depression can't fully catch me."

I have learned that I have to keep my heart, mind, spirit, and body moving. I am not sure if this is a key to longevity, but it sure makes life worth living.

Keeping It in Balance

On New Year's Day morning, you might be recovering from New Year's Eve events. The night before, maybe you had a toast or two with friends or met a new love; maybe you brought in the new year staying indoors, not wanting to be tomorrow's story, or you watched the ball fall in Times Square and eventually surrendered to slumber.

In the wee hours, I ventured out and stopped at Walgreen's to find some deals and pick up some miscellaneous items. I realized down the first aisle as I placed a card in the basket that it only had one handle.

As I tried to put another item in the rectangular bucket, I found that it didn't quite work the way I expected. I headed back to the front of the store to get a similar one with two handles. Much better.

It was quiet at 8:30 a.m. I noticed a man fumbling to get discounted Christmas/holiday candy into his fully functional basket, an employee sleepily stocking shelves, and a greeter who was truly excited about 2020. It was an eye-opening, exciting feeling to encounter people on the first day of the year. Realize I was also ecstatic because it was two degrees below zero and being inside gave me reason for mild celebration.

Some people comment that they have a lack of balance in their lives and are often frustrated. Although I try to maintain this equilibrium, I still have to revisit where I am, where I am going, and where I want to be. I might even be considered a poster child for "imbalance." Look up imbalance in the dictionary, and you might see my picture next to it. It depends on the edition you have.

Also, sometimes being imbalanced, like my experience with my first basket, make me appreciate the times when things seem just right or just so. Not everything works out as you intended, but sometimes you surprise yourself with a new insight when you fix your own basket or start over with a new one.

KOTEX Story

There was a time in my life where I used to write letters of recommendation for students going off to college. In this case, it was my second year at Academy of Holy Angels, where dreams become reality.

Anyway, before digital signatures, we would get the letters from the printer, sign them and send them off to the College and Career Center. I tried to set an example by using spellcheck to catch those occasional errors, but once I slipped big time. My last name is KOTZ, but somehow inadvertently, I hit the spelling option for KOTEX.

I think I caught most of them. But, to this day, I wonder how many of these fine college and university institutions received this embarrassing error of mine.

Life Is a Shitstorm

On a morning in September, I worked a Remembrance Walk in Stillwater, Minnesota. Our volunteer area was out of coffee, which helps fuel my energy helping with set up. Toward the end of a major task, I ambled over to a convenience store a block away from the scenic riverside.

I inquired of the store clerk, "How are you doing, man?"

"Shitty as ever," he chimed in a bad mood.

I said, "For me, a shot of java helps."

He said, "I see you like chuckwagons and donuts, too."

"Yes. A little early for a sandwich, but a donut with a coffee is one of the little pieces of heaven on earth."

"Life is still a shitstorm," he lamented. His eyes revealed sadness.

It made me think how many of us go through daily crises but do not express our distress as vociferously as this young man did.

I was able to witness the sunrise on a cool crisp morning; work with some awesome friends four years in the making; hear from a young couple about wedding plans and how they can get mixed up and become stressful in anticipation; saw some of my family at the remembrance event; saw a young lady from my high school teaching days, now a competent successful woman; saw people come together to work thorough some traumatic and heartbreaking grief; picked up some flowers for my wife and had her like my selection; talked with my neighbor about life in the big city of St. Paul; and came in the house to a dog that wanted to sit up on my shoulders—yes, not my lap, but my shoulders.

I thought back to that man expressing his woes and wished he could see just a few good glimpses of life.

The little things matter—and for me, even the chuckwagon.

Lights Out on the Golden Arches

After teaching an engaging class in Rochester, (which may be hard to believe when it runs from 5 p.m. to 10 p.m.), I met with a few students for feedback, then packed up and departed by around 10:20 p.m. After these classes, I feel a combination of fulfillment, exhaustion, and an adrenaline rush. At this time, exhaustion seems to win out, but I am often not quite sure.

I then realized I needed to drive home. Some nights, I stay overnight in the Rochester vicinity. The drive to St. Paul is about one and a half hours, and there are very few lights on the ride home. BUT this night, in trying to "resist a rest" and keep my eyes on the road for this journey, an iced coffee could make the difference.

The problem is that after 10 p.m. your options are limited on Highway 52. There is this one McDonald's, near Cannon Falls. I saw the Golden Arches in the distance, and said to myself, "I will make it to this drive-thru." It was around 10:55 p.m.

Just as I was ready to take the exit, by my watch, 10:59 p.m., the golden arches went dark. Minor fail. Now, I knew this place closed at 11 p.m.

It is funny how sometimes when you want something and you approach that viable option, occasionally the lights get turned off on you, and you just have to adjust.

Contrast of Light and Darkness

During a snowfall, I finished shoveling. Kali and I put lights on the bushes earlier in the day to get ready for the holidays, but they didn't work out as well as intended. Picture a combination of Sputnik-shaped stars and subtle frosted light-brown pinecone lights—but in the evening, the snow leveled the small shrubs, and the lights were covered.

For the last few years we had these five stars that twinkled and danced in the same area, but they were held up by little plastic posts which could withstand the weather. They finally lost their luster a week ago, as the fuse burned out. It was time to try something new.

I took the new luminaries and transferred them to the small maple. It is not a symmetric shaped tree by any means. It reminded me of a Charlie Brown type of tree—but the new lights lit up a small pocket of darkness on a dilapidated tree and gave joy to my daughter and me.

The contrast of light and darkness is an unusual gift.

Long-Distance Anniversary

When this vignette was written, I was in some tears. Not sad, but grateful. I write to you from Bogota. I can't fully explain my emotions, but it is my anniversary at this writing. My wife Jan and I celebrated twenty years today. I am very fortunate. That is one reason my eyes are swelling, as I write. In my past, I had a practice round earlier in marriage, so I reflect and know that in the grand scheme of things, life has given me abundance. I have been blessed with three talented, caring, and funny children, and have a dog who often seems to communicate like he's an actual person.

In Colombia, we had a young man who passed out in a classroom next door to mine. The professor asked me to come quickly. There was young Juan laying down on the floor. We called for help, and I talked with the young man to keep him conscious. I patted his face (he was a little clammy), and students gave me some cool water, and it seemed to soothe his face. You could see the students around him were quiet, but the love they had for him made a difference. He had enough water to drink, those in our orbit were holding his hand, and I told him, "I like your shirt," which had an image medley of someone looking like Bob Marley and Jimi Hendrix. He smiled. His eyes were clear.

In the end of this chapter, he ended up being just fine, a case of low blood sugar, but in my past not all has been fine. I have seen some incredibly difficult circumstances get worse.

As Juan was brought to his feet, Jorge (one of the multi-talented coordinators) and I brought him to the infirmary (nurse). Meanwhile, my own students got to have an extended break. I was grateful that this young man was okay, and at that moment Juan could continue with life, just like us.

Many of you do this so well. You see what you have been given, and you celebrate. For those that do not, take a moment and say to yourself, "I am lucky." You have life. It can be so fleeting. It can dissipate slowly, or end so quickly.

Loving People Bears Fruit

My daughter said, "Loving people always bears fruit." Often, it may not be reciprocated back directly to you, nor what you expect.

While walking the dog, a little boy and his mom approached us wearing a shirt that said, "I Am a Good Catch." He was fascinated with the dog, wanting to make a new friend, but then recoiled cautiously behind his mom's leg, assessing the situation.

I would like to think love is patient and kind. But, again, it may not come back to us in the way we anticipated.

On this beautiful evening, I was tired and a wee bit sad, trying to understand how to deal with a loved one losing their memory. Yet, the little boy and the little dog provided a conduit for me to see the love my daughter mentioned and the potential fruit it can bear.

The dog unconsciously revealed a smile to the boy, waving his front paws in excitement to his newfound friend. The boy, in turn, fully emerged from behind his mom's leg for an appropriate greeting, excited for the connection.

I do believe love radiates back to our own relationships, communities, and the world at large. Sometimes we get inundated with the vast complexities of life that we may not see it.

Seeing this little boy's glee in the simplicity of making a possible connection with another mammal his size made me smile, and for the moment took me out of my own thoughts and sensitivities, recognizing that "love does bear much fruit"—in our case, for both people and animals.

Maybe I Need an Upgrade

On a beautiful sunny morning, I met a good friend for a walk at Lake Como. Not too far into our stride, we hit a few puddles, and as we walked along the preformed paths in the snow surrounding the water, a set of keys to a Lexus sat propped on the path.

For more than a moment, I thought about upgrading to a new car with this newfound high-end set of keys. My Dodge Dart had served me well, but this was my opportunity to move up a few notches in my life with a luxury vehicle. At least, the thought did cross my mind. Competing with this was another thought of going to prison, and the idea that someone was actually searching for these keys. I quickly came back to reality.

The Pavilion was closed, with Dockside having changed ownership in the past year. It might have been a good place to drop off the keys, since we were a stone's throw away.

Instead, we decided to pick them up and continue on our walk. We asked a few individuals if they lost any keys. Eventually, fifteen minutes later, a runner told us a man was waiting anxiously in the parking lot to get into his car. We could see him from across the lake.

When we reached the man, he looked nervous. He was holding a couple of Lincoln dollar denominations in his outstretched hand, and said, "Thank you! Here. Keep this."

I said, "No, sir. Not necessary. Keep the change."

He mentioned that he had slipped on his own walk and went "ass over tea kettle," not realizing his keys had flown into the snow.

"Can I buy you a drink, then?" he offered.

My friend and I laughed and declined the generous offer.

He looked relieved, and my fellow walker and I exchanged a few more stories and went on to our own lives.

Maybe I could have given the Lexus a test drive, before handing over the keys?

Maybe Once Is Enough

"You only live once, but if you do it right, once is enough." Mae West

Moving Through Life

"As you move through this life and this world you change things slightly, you leave marks behind, however small. And in return, life—and travel—leaves marks on you. Most of the time, those marks—on your body or on your heart—are beautiful. Often, though, they hurt." Anthony Bourdain

My Shift Ends Soon

I headed to a store to pick up some items my family needed, and fielded a special request for my wife, because we were out of milk. I decided to go through the self-checkout, where there was an enclosed area with six stations to scan your own items.

I waited in line. When I got to my station, everything was going smoothly, and each item registered the price.

Then, I hit a small blip. I mentioned to the checkout associate that the grocery sign said I could get six yogurts for the price of five, but it wasn't ringing up on the monitor.

I asked her how her day was going, and she helped me process a discount of $1.39.

"Thank you!" I beamed, excited about my meager savings.

She smiled, and then revealed to me, "So many people have attitudes."

It made me think back to the time I was in a completely different store venue to return a CD, and someone perturbed in front of me was returning a TV, because the picture clarity was so bad.

Apparently, the customer sales agent told the buyer returning this item that they forgot to remove the protective film coating on the set, and that this may have accounted for the resolution being blurry. The customer insisted that was not the problem, and the TV was returned, all while the customer service agent was so patient, and handled the paperwork for the return with no drama.

I flashed back to the present.

"Well, I hope I am not adding to the difficulties!" I said and commiserated with her on this Sunday afternoon, where shoppers were plentiful.

"No. You were a piece of cake."

"Don't let the cranky ones get you down," I said, exiting with my two bags.

"My shift ends pretty soon," and she gave me a tired smile.

Navigating Life

Navigating the ice patches around Como Lake with a dog can be a mildly harrowing experience. This day, I took one tumble, as Jake wanted to sprint through a small temporary pond, while I tried to stay on the ice shoreline. A slip, and in an instant I was in a snowbank on Wheelock Parkway bike path, while the little dog stared at me, wondering why we were stopping so abruptly.

At the pavilion, I met a man who wondered whether we would again have another restaurant owner within this historic building. We will call him Mr. D. He explained that he was in an airborne division during the Vietnam War.

He trained many men in Georgia on their way to Vietnam, and said that when the young men came back from one service period, they often experienced bad PTSD, and due to the use of drugs to combat the pain, as well as other reasons, often impaired many of our servicemen's judgement.

He mentioned that our government could have done a much better job taking care of our servicemen and women. He acknowledged back then that even though it was a contentiously debated war, we left many of these men and women without the emotional support they needed to re-enter the society that we all take for granted.

After a brief reflection, we also laughed that as we both progress in age that one tumble on some ice can alter your life. My good fortune landed me in a snowbank. Next time, I might wear some padding and possibly a helmet with a chinstrap.

Olu or Oly

I was trying diligently to write an email to one of my students named "Olu." I tried a few times, and it kept changing his first name to "Oly." On the fourth attempt, it stayed in the wrong version.

For a second, I thought the Gmail system was trying to make the effort to permanently change his name! (Without a doubt, this is a first-world problem, but it made me laugh).

Ridiculous

In an Austin airport men's room, near the line of sinks, I hear a guy who just washed his hands yell out, "Where are the #$kand% towels?!"

I chuckled to myself and explained to the man that the dryer is part of the same system as the hand wash.

I showed him how it worked, having been befuddled by this technology on an earlier trip.

He gave me a surprised look, and said, "That's #$kand% ridiculous!" and walked out.

Sinkhole

Today, my neighbor yelled from across the street, "I see you have a sinkhole." He was right.

Who knew we would have a 3 foot by 2 foot crater develop in our front yard? After a trip to a garden center, and using about 70 to 100 pounds of dirt, filler and topsoil, I think we finally have it filled. But time will tell.

I said to my neighbor, "If you see me disappear while cutting the grass, you'll know where I went."

Sitting at the Pazzaluna Bar

I decided to go downtown to Pazzaluna and sit at the bar. On this Friday, where just about everyone is out of town, at the cabin, or watching Netflix, I was craving a margherita pizza, a couple meatballs, and a cabernet. It happened to be a Castle Rock wine, which was just what the doctor ordered. On another night, if it were not for the Italian fare, I might have had an ice-cold Summit pale ale, but this combination was fixed in my mind, and it became a reality.

In the vicinity, St. Paul's Rice Park looks refreshingly inviting, after a series of construction touches. Parking is a couple bucks at the meters and is usually easy to find at this time of year.

Sitting facing all the liquors and spirits, a younger guy was chatting up some ladies, and I was watching the highlights of the US Women's soccer team, with discussion ensuing among the commentators of the upcoming match against the Netherlands. The younger guy was also eyeing my solo pizza. I offered him a piece, and he proceeded to tell me that he was losing his job in August as a journalist, and as a forty-year-old, he was unsure of his future. He didn't take me up on the offer of a slice.

We discussed Central and South America, in relation to the US, economically and politically, and no one started yelling.

I also mentioned that he would find something in his line of work, and told him that when I moved past the half-century milestone, I became more reflective, less judgmental, and more able to approach life's twists and turns as a "sitcom."

Realize that a very wise person told me about this, and I decided to pass on the knowledge to this guy. I continued, "Sometimes observing with bemusement and laughter can get you through some rough spots, maybe even save your life."

At this point, the guy asked me if my offer still stood about the slice of pizza, and I said, "It is all yours, man."

The bartender lamented having a rough night, working this shift alone due to a colleague who didn't make it because of a death in the family. I finally got her to smile, asking her if she "blew off firecrackers in late June through July 4th just to annoy neighbors."

She laughed and told me that in her neighborhood, "it actually happens." I paid my bill, and she said, "Have a great night!"

The journalist next to me who devoured my last slice, quipped, "Hope you have a sh$kky night. I hope you wake up with your clothes on!"

I smiled, and knew it was time to go. "Sending you good vibes on that next career move. Something will come through."

With a glazed look, he said, "Thanks, boss, for the pizza."

Soon I Will Be Able to Hide My Own Easter Eggs

Yesterday, I went to fill up my tank at SA (now Speedway), went inside to purchase some food items, and the friendly clerk said, "Do you have your SA card?" I flashed my bar code on my keychain, exchanged an excited comment about getting a free donut, collected my bag of items, and exited. Back at the car, I discovered that I could not find my keys.

Funny, I didn't remember being absent-minded. I checked my front pockets frantically. "Maybe I left them in the car?!" No luck. "Life is now officially unfair." I went back in to check with the clerk, and people were waiting in line. "Did anyone see some keys on the counter?" I asked.

Someone remarked, "He lost his keys." No luck. I felt a heightened sense of panic. I was thinking, *If all is not lost, where are my keys?!*

I went back outside, and as I checked my front pockets one more time, I tried my back pocket and they magically appeared. "What? I never put my keys there!" Relief settled in. Soon, I will be able to hide my own Easter eggs.

She Is the Most Beautiful Woman in the World

At the Minneapolis Vets Home, once a week, I bring those who served our country back and forth in wheelchairs from their rooms to physical rehab. Many of these men and women are suffering from dementia or the onset of Alzheimer's. This morning, I was bringing back a dear man, who had been in the Battle of the Bulge, who repeatedly asks his age, (during transport) back to rehabilitation: "How old am I?"

"You're ninety-two."

"Where am I?"

"You're in Building 6. We're headed to Building 19."

"What's there?"

"Rehab."

"Damn, it's cold in here."

"Yes, it's worse outside." I say. "It's so cold that cows voluntarily line up to get branded." He laughs heartily and then asks me how old he is, again.

Next, I bring back an ambulatory female vet from rehab to her room. She always wants to be walked back to her room like she is going to prom. On our way back, I pick up another vet, who is screaming at me: "I ain't going to rehab two days in a row. Stop right here." A nurse kindly lets me know she will take him back to the game room, where he initially was.

Then, I bring another vet (new to me), named Don, back to his room. "Where is my wife?" he asks.

"I am not sure."

"What time is it?"

"It's 9:15 a.m."

"She'll be here at lunch. I know it. She is the most beautiful woman in the world."

"I imagine she would be, Don. What is her name?"

"Martha. Is she here, yet?"

I finally get him up to the third floor to drop him off, and the nurses (probably from hearing his same story), roll their eyes, but smile. Don proudly states once again: "She is the most beautiful woman in the world."

I say to him: "That's your story, Don. And I bet you're sticking to it!"

Martha is not there. At least not, yet.

What struck me most is his indelible memory of a person so dear to him, (even while suffering dementia): "She is the most beautiful woman in the world." That's a specific memory worth saving, which I hope he never loses.

We Have a Good Story to Tell

We all have a story to tell. Back in May of 2000, I had been hired to teach in a high school in the Twin Cities. I was scheduled to teach World and American History, and a couple of math courses.

My dad had passed away earlier the month before, and the excitement and fear of the unknown—a new environment—awaited me in August.

Life has a way of taking what you expected to happen and turning it into something you were intended to do—at least for a moment in time.

A couple of weeks before the school year started, the geometry teacher, who taught three sections, had taken a new position in the prison system. My principal strongly suggested that this position needed to be filled, and knew I had the license. A typical load for most teachers of high school is five or six classes, and some supervision expectations like a study hall or something similar are part of your daily routine.

It appeared after our discussion that I would not teach history, but would be teaching mathematics—five sections, including the three geometry courses left vacant. I was a little disappointed and deflated, but adjusted to the task at hand. I thought this assignment would be temporary.

In fact, this temporary assignment was an adjustment I ended up making for the next thirteen years—doing something that I did not initially expect, but maybe at the time I was intended to do.

I found a way to incorporate history and news into daily lessons about mathematics, and today, even though this experience is in the rear view mirror for me, it served as an invaluable epoch that I did not intend to happen.

This morning I heard a story about a man relaying stories to his children about his own father. His dad had passed away before his own children could get to know this "Papa Pete." He would tell stories that his dad told him, and the kids would be intrigued, laugh, and want another tale about their grandpa.

Unbeknownst to the son who told tales of and about his dad, an unexpected discovery unfolded a new mystery. In checking a roof leak, he discovered a box the size of a treasure chest in the attic. Manuscript after manuscript. Papers and letters. Papa Pete loved to write.

Relatives had some inkling of this, and Pete was considered accomplished in some circles. But there was this magic box with some of the stories that he had been telling his own kids.

It occurred to me that many of those stories were untold.

Maybe it is better that way. Some things are better left unsaid.

But you have your own story that is unfolding right before your own eyes. Your own story could capture someone's heart, maybe make it beat a bit faster. Maybe it will change someone's life for the better.

What Scares You?

Yesterday, someone asked me, "What scares you the most about the future?"

I had to think about this, but for me it is the "fear of the unknown." Not knowing what may lie ahead, good or bad or somewhere in between, is harder for me to deal with than it is for the average person. Yet, how I manage this fear is taking each day one a time, being present to the goodness—and often greatness—I see right in front of me.

Laughing and finding the humor in daily life helps me, too. One of my best friends told me if you approach life as a sitcom, you don't take it as seriously, when adversity or difficult situations arise.

I am not saying that life is one big comedy or laugh track, but there are plenty of events that happen each day where laughter may be a better tonic or medicine than reacting negatively.

The same person who asked me about fear earlier, pressed me with what "my five-year plan" is, and I had to laugh, since I have some thoughts about my future but truly do not know the answer to this. I acknowledged that it is a good question, but for now I have to live in the moment, because I truly do not know what God or life has in store for me.

Hopefully, your life continues to be an adventurous surprise filled with more joy, fewer roadblocks, less sorrow, and more opportunities for growth.

Would You Fill Out a Survey?

There is plenty that I do not understand in our world. So, I approach the small things with diligence and wonder. Today, I called our power company because of a discrepancy on our bill. The customer service agent reviewed the account and found that they made an error, so I would get a refund check. How often does that happen?

As he was waiting to make an adjustment to the account by his computer, I told him that I was so glad I could have some extra cash in my pocket, because I was taking my wife out for her birthday today.

He laughed, and said, "Glad I could help."

I said, "Do you know how to remember your wife's birthday?"

He responded, "I don't know. How?"

"Just forget it once," I quipped.

He laughed some more, and I heard the phone drop.

After a pause, he said, "I did that before."
"What did you do before?" I inquired.
"I forgot."
"How did that work out for you?"
"Not so good. But I ALWAYS remember now!"
Then I laughed.

After my account was cleared up, the customer service professional said, "Now that we are friends, would you wait on the line to fill out a customer survey?"

#381

For lunch, I was craving a quarter-pounder with cheese, and a mocha frappé. The juicy burger McDonald's makes "fresh" is tastier, and the frappe is like a shot of crack—a sugar-filled liquid happy pill in a cup. Maybe not the healthiest choice.

The drive-through was crowded, so I decided to dine in at the fine establishment on University. I asked for the frappé without the whip. The woman who was making the drink was busy but was an artist at her job.

She queried, "Sir, did you say 'no whip'?"

I opened with, "Vanessa—yes. Thanks for asking. I love this drink on warm days."

As she twirled around a little stressed, she said, "These are good. Like a dessert. How did you know my name?!"

I offered, "You are famous around here. Plus, your name tag helped."

She quipped, "I am not famous. But my name is!"

"How is your day going?" I asked, still waiting for my juicy burger.

"I am waiting for my shift to be over, soon. Here's that drink. No whip," she said with a smile. Another guy yelled out, "#381. Quarter-pounder with cheese!"

"Thanks, man."

On my receipt, it asked me to fill out a survey, and after it was completed, I would receive a validation code to redeem a "buy one get one free" item to use within thirty days.

I thought, *Why not?*

I signed in by entering a numeric code which was at least twelve digits long. The survey was rather lengthy, and asked about the quality of food, atmosphere, service, and "Would you come back again?" Plus, there was a comment section.

At the same time, I finished off both delectable items, received my validation code from my survey, and ready to depart, noticed Vanessa among the other hard-working McDonald's employees making another flavored coffee. I said, "Just so you know...I filled out the customer survey. It took me a while, but I told them you are a gem! I hope they let you know. Thank you!"

She was a barista in motion, but she stopped in her tracks, appearing to be a little teary-eyed, but seemed happy.

Upon leaving, I said, "No need to cry. You don't want tears in the coffee, now do you?"

She laughed, and said, "My shift is over! Thanks."

It made me want to fill out another customer survey to get a delicious juicy burger, and also to see someone else be recognized.

Leadership

Simple Measures

As many of you know, the documentary *Won't You Be My Neighbor?* was in theaters throughout the US. When I was a kid, I used to watch some of the episodes from the original show *Mister Rogers' Neighborhood* and listen to the "Won't you be my neighbor?" song with some glee and anticipation for what he might say and do next.

As I grew up, some people thought and I as a teenager (who now knew everything) turned the tables on Fred, and believed he was a naive man, who needed to get a grip, and face reality for what it is—a fast-moving, sometimes callous, uncaring world where monetary gain and success are what truly matter.

But Fred Rogers was on to something. He would put that sweater on (which seemed excessive on hot days) and jump into a life lesson for children, and possibly some adults, too.

He would change his shoes, and according to David Brooks, "gently give children obvious and nonobvious advice: You are special just the way you are; no, children can't fall down the drains in the bathtub."

Sometimes he would slow down time and be silent for long periods as he fed his fish.

Brooks continued to explain, "Occasionally he touched on politics. During the civil rights era, when black kids were being thrown out of swimming pools, Rogers and a black character bathed their feet together in a tub." Brotherhood. We as people, in a small wading pool.

After Bobby Kennedy was killed, Rogers gently explained what an assassination was.

Rogers once asked a young man with a major disability to pray for him. The kid was shocked, because usually people want to pray for the young man, the child with challenges.

But, once again Mr. Rogers saw that someone who had more daily struggles than he did, was actually closer to God and could provide a better chance at intercession than he could. Plus, he might have boosted that kid's self-esteem in immeasurable ways.

In his subtle and gentle style, Fred Rogers was a hero. He made it clear that we all can take simple measures to make the world a better place.

A Wake-Up Call

When someone confides in you, I consider it a blessing and a curse. On the one hand, you want to be a decent human being and (within reason) look out for your fellow man or woman by listening, not judging, and showing empathy. To me, it is a blessing when you can be there for a friend.

On the other hand, sensitive information sent your way can almost seem too personal and overwhelming to hear. And the dilemma or troubling situation may be revealed in an uncomfortable way and may not be something you can help the person who confides in you bring to a resolution.

In *The 50th Law*, Robert Greene stated, "Mentally framing a negative event as a blessing in disguise makes it easier for you to move forward."

I also maintain that at times, not getting what you want may be a stroke of luck.

I have often found that when I face some negative event, or something temporarily debilitating, I need to reach out to others I can trust for a refreshed perspective.

Well, I had an individual ask to meet and they expressed that they were going through some painful marital issues, job stresses, family strife among multiple sides of families, feelings of losing their center and purpose, and feeling rather hopeless.

Some of you may find at times that at least one of those categories fit you, too!

After mentioning that we all have some cross to bear, sharing some of my own experiences of being befuddled, and somehow with a mentor, and I believe with God's guidance, I emerged a better person—so too could this person experiencing copious troubling life issues emerge out of their own temporary situation of desperation, and see their own self-worth. Also, a good night's rest can help you see the situation clearly. Revisiting life's challenges when you are refreshed can make a major difference.

Negative or temporarily debilitating events can truly be a wakeup call for us to see what we are made of, where our heart is guiding us, and where we can possibly alter our future course in the chapter tomorrow.

Ask Him About Dogs

I was told by the therapists that John was very volatile at times, but if you talked about dogs, he would willingly acquiesce and come with you to therapy. He had refused earlier that morning.

"What the hell do you want?!"

"John—I am here to take you to PT."

"When?"

"Soon. Your appointment is in ten minutes. Hey, do you like dogs?"

And then John became eagerly animated, describing how "you can trust these animals more than people." He pointed out all the pictures on his wall of the different dogs he owned, and therapy canines who came to visit at the veterans' home. He told me about Anoka, and how his family had raised rabbits, and when they brought bunnies to his room, they climbed all over him, because these little creatures knew he "would never hurt them, and use them for a stew."

His chest of drawers had a hat sitting on top that said, "Hero—Vietnam." It was covered by another picture of Manny, a dog who never left his side, even when he had the defining stroke that brought John here in the first place.

"Yeah. Manny was my favorite. You could have a large bag of treats to pry him away from a bastard like me, but he would never leave my side. You don't see people who will stick by you nowadays."

"Who the &!%* are you again?! Don't tell me. Pauly? I have seen you before." With a mischievous grin, he said, "Let's play hide and seek. You go hide, and no one will come find you." And then he and I laughed.

"Well, if you don't come find me, you will not get to work with one of the wonderful physical therapists this morning." I quipped back.

He relented. "I guess we better go down." Together, we addressed the wheelchair. He backed in, and we rode to our destination ten minutes away.

The therapist gave me a knowing look when we arrived. Without a word, she instinctively knew what happened, and didn't seem to mind that we were late.

Balancing Balls

Imagine life is a game in which you are juggling five balls. The balls are called work, family, health, friends, and integrity. And you're keeping all of them in the air. But one day you finally come to understand that work is a rubber ball. If you drop it, it will bounce back. The other four balls are made of glass. If you drop one of these, it will be irrevocably scuffed, nicked, perhaps even shattered. And once you truly understand the lesson of the five balls, you will have the beginnings of balance in your life.

Being Too Nice

Can you be too nice?

In my line of work, I make the attempt daily to be nice. But the reality is that quite often, tough things need to be said. This is not easy for me, but based on experience, and myriad mistakes I have made myself, it is better to give a person some options so they can make better decisions, or so they don't keep hurting themselves or others. (One disclaimer: I have gotten pretty good at giving others options and advice but also need guidance in steering my own ship.)

Most of us would agree that kindness is a virtue. But, when you are too nice, some of the pitfalls are that:

LEADERSHIP

1. People will start to consider you to be weak. Keeping it brief, people may think you do not have a backbone, and you do not have the strength to confront adversity or difficult issues.
2. You often may forget to be nice to yourself. Givers often deplete their good energy and then feel drained. Maybe taking some time for yourself to recharge would benefit even more individuals that you would truly like to serve.
3. You attract the wrong kind of people. You become this magnet for people to stick to and take advantage of. This can be good at times, but you also need someone or groups to consider your needs, too.
4. Some people will mistrust you. I have heard this one throughout my life. As an example, in the corporate world, I was having a good day, and was smiling ebulliently while walking down the hallway. In my small euphoria, someone sniped me with, "You smile too much. You must not have much to do!" Ouch. I still think you should still try to be happy, but not everyone wants to see you joyous, or they consider this something you should not flaunt.
5. You might possibly warp your own expectations. Nice people give and often take on people's problems, and they should be commended. But then the unrealistic expectation can eventually kick in that "people should be nice to them." I wish it could be this way. But the reality is that this may be what your mind and heart needs. It may not be someone else's need.

Cognizance of Kindness

I have had a few friends confide in me that they have broken off contact with a longtime friend, because they have different beliefs or attitudes, or because something in their lives just changed.

It is hard when you get dumped or dropped. It is often swift, painful, and you feel blind-sided. At the same time, some of you are as tough as nails and say to yourself, "It is just one less person to deal with." I have to admit that my own clock does not tick like the latter sentiment.

I recognize that we all grow, change, often go our own ways in life, and this is natural. Not everyone is easy to relate to. Maybe they once were, but you do not see eye to eye in the present. Some of us crave the past and want to make everything right again.

Often, it doesn't happen. Disappointing, right?

I have amazing neighbors. They are kind, live their own lives, and help you when you need it. We share resources, ideas, shovel each other's walks, and banter about all of the ash trees we recently lost.

I have friends and colleagues who look out for me, especially when I am in need of a boost. In my line of work, I mentor, sponsor, and advocate for others. But someone once told me that "to be a good mentor, you also need a mentor." True that. I am grateful for those who guide me, give me feedback on what I do well, and coach me when I may miss critical insights or need a lifeline.

I have family that make me very happy. That does not mean it is always reciprocal, or fifty-fifty. Was it ever meant to be? I miss my daughters and stepson, but when we do get together, it is that much better. I am thankful for the time I do have and wish I had more, but have accepted dealing with the reality of life.

We all must find our own way in the world, and letting go to see the next stages is often emotional for me—mostly joyous! I may want more time with my grown-up kids, friends, and siblings, but the reality is that they have their own movie to act out.

Losing a connection or bond with someone you love or loved is difficult and sometimes unexplainable. Often that person of significance has another chapter to act out or complete. Yes, sometimes it is due to both of you parting ways due to differences or direction, but often it was just meant to be.

I wish it could be kinder, and I continue to observe we need more of this vital virtue, but consider this: Letting go and celebrating what you experienced in your past has made you the fine, unique person you are today. Hopefully, the person you are now never releases their own cognizance of kindness. Hold on to that.

LEADERSHIP

Day in the Life of a Teacher

I love my job as a teacher. I teach an MBA course which is considered very difficult and also intimidating for students, who are dealing with decision analysis.

Anyway, I have been through this territory before, and guide the students so hopefully they believe in themselves and come out better decision-makers.

Last night, it was frenetic and people seemed stressed from their work days. Before class, one of my international students was trying to schedule an appointment on some automated system on their phone for September 33rd. "Oh. It is not available. How about the 31st?" (Did I miss the memo? Are there now additional days in this month?)

Another student came to see me at the break and said he could not see the board, but is trying to afford some glasses, but he has no health plan, and cash flow is low. I told him we can have him sit in front, and I will make my slides larger for him.

Another individual commented in class, "If all the material is like this, I will definitely fail."

I assured all of them, "If I can do it, you can too."

One individual sincerely asked, "For this week, are all problems posted on Blackboard? I do not have the book."

"Yes, they are." (We did go over this a few times, but patience is a virtue, and I have yet to fully master it.)

"I still do not have the book yet. I ordered it on Amazon. Can you photocopy all of the problems and post these electronically?!"

"Well, without the book, you might have some issues," I lamented. I said, "You can borrow mine for this week."

"That is okay, Professor—it is too heavy for my bag."

Finally, another one of my students came up for more explanation at the end of class, and remarked, "This is fascinating. But I do not get it. Can you revisit the window and door manufacturing problem from start to finish?"

Again, I thought, *I love my job.*

Don't Wait to Try

A wise person said to me: "Don't wait. Don't wait to try something, to initiate, to take action. Stop playing it safe or looking for someone else to take the lead. Be a creative creator of your life. You can make it as exciting and thrilling as you wish."

Doors Opening

"If you've tried everything possible to get an outcome and it just hasn't worked out as planned, stop trying so hard. Relax. Maybe the timing's not right. Maybe it wasn't in your best interests. Maybe while one door seems to be closing, another is opening." (Robin S. Sharma)

"Sometimes we stare so long at a door that is closing that we see too late the one that is open." (Alexander Graham Bell)

"Sometimes in life, when we really want something, we can approach it in a way that might actually be closing us off from achieving it." (Gretchen Bleiler)

"At the end of your life, you will never regret not having passed one more test, not winning one more verdict or not closing one more deal. You will regret time not spent with a husband, a friend, a child, or a parent." (Barbara Bush)

Doug Landry

Doug, one of my first bosses, was known for his integrity, mentoring others, and helping to develop and lead the reinsurance division.

In studying for exams to be an actuary, he encouraged me, "If I can do it, anyone can."

Doug was measured, sensible, and down to earth. He got along with virtually everyone. He had no airs about him.

We would do an experience review for one of our Eastern reinsurance clients, and Doug would tell me: "You saved us money in that last review. But you need to never forget to wear a belt, and it is also important to zip up your fly." It was an indelible lesson learned. And, then he would start to laugh in such a way that you didn't feel small for making mistakes.

Doug was a terrific example. He mentored you when you needed guidance, and he had the ability to laugh and enjoy life, even in the toughest times, when a critical decision needed to be made. He also introduced me to cigars and knew how to take time to celebrate successes.

The class, humility, and manner in which he treated others was a lesson not lost on me nor on all the lives he touched.

He was an extraordinary human being who is still missed by many and forgotten by none.

I am a better person because of Doug.

Expressing Your Essence

The dolphin has limitations. Among other things, it cannot swim on the land for long durations, run a business, or learn Spanish in school. Maybe, it is checking out what life has to offer above the surface, possibly searching for a delicious meal, or could it be that the dolphin is just happy to stand up straight and be proud of what it is?

Whatever it may be, this wondrous creature is expressing its own essence but may not know its full capability.

Blakeley said, "Don't be intimidated by what you don't know. That can be your greatest strength and ensure that you do things differently from everyone else."

Feedback

Giving and getting feedback in person is a gratifying part of being a teacher and of mentoring. I also get comments on what I am doing well, and where I can improve. It is not always easy, a little exhausting, but it is meaningful, and to me, a gift.

Last night, after class had ended, I had one student who wanted to discuss their current journey. It was filled with frustration, fear of not being able to get the job she wanted, being excluded, being consciously aware of her talents, acknowledging that she needed patience and that it was hard to wait for the next good opportunity in her life.

I listened, gave her a connection to someone better suited to advise her, told her of experiences I have had, and eventually brought the meeting to closure. I assured her of her talents, her keen abilities, and that she had value.

This person had some previous hurt built up and was struggling to find her own meaning in the present.

I get it. Life is filled with questions, and answers are often hard to come by.

I said to her: "Picture your heart as something that can hold only so much emotion, and when a certain percent of it is filled with frustration and fear, that portion cannot easily accept anything good. While that might be an odd thing to imagine, it is basically what you're doing when you allow a previous hurt to cloud your present life."

She paused. Then she broke down, revealed that she is in pain for a variety of reasons, and said after some emotional wrangling, "Thank you."

As I have seen time and time again, it is a gift for me to be able to temporarily steer someone in a positive direction. On occasion, I may open, as an unintended consequence, Pandora's Box. Mythology still holds that hope remains inside.

At times, I too struggle with the same sense of inadequacy and uncertainty. Often, I am not so sure that I actually help in many instances, but I do try.

The good thing is that we are all in this together. Sometimes, it takes someone else to help us see our own developing selves in a clear light.

Giving Up the Peanut Butter Bar

In early December, I was halfway through an eight-week course with graduate students. We typically finish at 9:30 p.m., and after addressing a few student questions and concerns, and as everyone was clearing out, one particular individual asked, "Can I talk to you for a minute?"

This look was not the kind that implied "I need help in your course with the subject matter," but had the signs of "I need to talk with someone."

"Sure. What's up?"

I listened and found that the myriad problems were outside my skill set, but this wasn't the first time. I taught high school for fifteen years, and for my colleagues and friends in this arena at any age level, my hat is off to you. There are too many of you to mention. Thank you for being there, in those unexpected moments.

In this case, I was confronted by family woes; pressures at work; one of her own sons was out of control with unpredictable hormones; a newly acquired driving permit for the other daughter, which worried the mom; a boyfriend who was aggressive; and in describing the story, the individual who asked if we could talk had eyes that began to swell with tears. Some of the other unmentioned issues made me want to cry. But I stayed strong.

"Do you want some of my almonds? I also still have this chocolate peanut butter bar. You can have some of this," I said. (My motto: "Break the ice with food when tears develop.")

She swayed away from the almonds but chose my square peanut butter bar with the thin layer of chocolate on the top. For some reason, this treat is sought after. (For a split second, I was sorry I offered, because I was a bit peckish, and I like these.)

I opened up the package. "Thanks," she said as she munched on my after-class night-time snack.

Sure enough, twenty minutes went by. It was now 10:00, and security popped their head in the door, giving me hand signals that we needed to make a motion toward leaving the building very soon.

I reflected that sometimes all the training you go through to be a content expert is eclipsed by the on-demand interpersonal skills needed to listen to people's life issues in a humane way.

Maya Angelou once said, "In the end, it is not necessarily what you have said to a person that makes a difference. It is how you make them feel."

I think I was able to give some possible assistance and a referral for some other qualified help that could possibly benefit this person, but in the end I lost most of my peanut butter bar. And, you know what? I have no idea if I did any good.

Somehow, the individual's daily life complexities of pain may have been relieved for a brief instant by listening, for the most part. She at least left the room with her chin up.

But in the end, the person walked out to the parking lot with security, and I had a few of my almonds before I packed up and headed home.

Help Me to Be a Better Man

Recently, one of my students said, "How do you remain flexible with us, when we can be so difficult?" It made me reflect on something I say to myself almost every day.

When I wake up, I ask, "God, help me be a better man."

My wife has also prayed with me, "PLEASE help him be a better man."

Before I walk into the door of every classroom I teach, I often say, "Help me be a good teacher today. Help me bring kindness, clarity, laughter, and joy to people. Help me heal and never hurt...." This prayer and mantra do not always work, and I often just fail, but it does put me in a better frame of mind to approach the complexities of the day.

It Won't Be Easy

I am currently reading a book about teaching. It is called, *It Won't Be Easy*, by Tom Rademacher. It is exceedingly honest, and some will think, as he indicated, "slightly unprofessional," but it shared his perspective on what it is like to face the young adolescent masses each and every day.

Teaching is messy and often just plain unpredictable. Each day is filled with joy, pain, mysteries, and surprises.

Right now, as we approach the New Year, some of you are getting ready for a snowstorm, catching up on sleep, and telling bad jokes like "The guy who developed the Band-Aid was a bloody genius."

Maybe you just had a deep connected discussion with a dear friend or someone you are newly reconnected to; maybe you are contemplating the odds of the Vikings making the playoffs; some of you are listening to smooth jazz. Or none of the above

Meanwhile, I am thinking back to an incident years ago, from one of my days of high school teaching.

There was this kid who "almost cheated" on an exam for another class. I think about the patient, merciful female teacher who asked me (on my way to lunch) to take the young man into the men's room and have him remove the ink off his inner thigh, so he didn't have an advantage for an upcoming exam in the afternoon.

The teacher also asked me to give the young man a "talking-to."

The best I could muster up at the time was, "Life is not easy, and although your attempt to cheat was creative, having answers on your inner thigh while wearing shorts is not the wisest move."

I continued, "Do you realize how lucky you are that Ms. So-and-So did not fully bust you, and failed you for this exam or have you removed from school?!"

"Uh. Yes, sir."

"You cheated but technically haven't followed through as of yet, because you will remove this ink. Take the soap from the dispenser, go in the stall, and wash it all away. Here, take these towels."

"Okay. Sorry."

"Did you really have to have the Ten Commandments on your leg, too?! Next time, you should have these memorized!"

"Yeah. I guess."

The bell rang, and in all the excitement, I missed lunch.

"I am not sure what is going to happen, but be sure to thank that teacher for what she did for you. She saved you. Not everyone gets that chance. Wash the ink off your hands, too. Here is another towel."

"Sorry." Head down.

"Do something good. Alright?"

"Okay, Mr. Kotz."

"Don't be late." My stomach growled at me, as I growled at the kid.

I always wonder if this was a pivotal moment for this young man to change his ways. Or not. Maybe he now is making a living selling fake tickets or using someone's identity to become a multi-millionaire through illicit means.

Or not. I am going to assume he is doing good work in the world, and this was just a small blip of bad judgement.

Thank you to the teachers I have had the pleasure to work with (and those I have never met) who do their best with the countless experiences they have daily—with your kids.

I am also glad there are people who believe in second chances for kids to see their mistakes, and to learn from them. When people believe in us, we grow into better people.

It's a Great Life if You Know When to Weaken

My dad passed away in April of 2000. I still wonder what he would think of the world today.

When I was a young buck, he would often say things like...

"What do you know for sure?" I would often be dumbfounded as to the answer.

"It is a great life if you know when to weaken." (*What the hell does this mean?* I often reflected.)

And when I was adamant as a teen, and ready to move out, "You will never realize how smart I am until you are thirty-five!" Yeah... okay.

Now, I think I comprehend the one question and statements more fully.

What do I know for sure? Everyone has some goodness in them. Sometimes you have to dig deep to find it.

Secondly, you will never get everything you want in life. You have to pick your battles, know when to let go, and let God guide you.

Third, I now "get" some of the wisdom my dad had. As a teen

LEADERSHIP

I thought I had all the answers. Now, I have a few but am still on a journey. And I am way past thirty-five.

Lesson Learned in the Cafeteria

I will never forget the young lady who teachers said "would never amount to much," who was disruptive in high school class but misunderstood, was made fun of by other kids because she was considered overweight, who had a tough home life that not many knew about, and who wasn't considered the ideal student. But she had this mischievous, yet good-natured smile. I always liked this kid, who is now an adult.

In the days when we used milk tickets, I noticed a young guy who either forgot his tickets/money or didn't have any that day. He was fumbling through his pockets, but came up with some fuzz, a faded sticker, and a Band-Aid. But there was no cash for lunch.

Monitoring a lunchroom is not my favorite activity, but on that day, I saw that same young lady, discredited by others, give up her money and milk tickets to that young man. She expected nothing in return, gave him a smile and money for a meal, and then proceeded to sit alone in the lunchroom.

Later, I told her that what she did helped that young guy, who I noticed had trouble with being short on funds, and how she had made his day. I cajoled her over to an area where there were other young ladies and asked the kids less inclined to be inclusive to "make a new friend."

She insightfully said to me later, at the young age of fifteen, "I didn't want him to feel the embarrassment I feel at home when we cannot have dinner, some nights."

And, then I became thankful that I worked the lunchroom that day, and for the lesson in kindness she taught me.

National Compliment Day

Every day, I hope we find someone to appreciate. January 24th happens to be "National Compliment Day." I learned this morning that the word "compliment" is derived from the Latin "complere," which means "to fill up."

This morning was frenetic, and it was definitely "filled up" with unusual occurrences. In my transport duties, I had one vet who broke out in convulsions while in his wheelchair and another who broke his foot pad; one veteran was snoring so loudly that he made a raucous horn sound like you were in the middle of an AC/DC song.

I was also able to help a therapist using an Allen wrench to fix one of the arm rests; and finally, on my way out, a lady jumped out of her car to tell me how irritated she was because there were no parking spots left in the lot. She asked if I was leaving, and I said I was. She then changed her mind, and told me how upset and frustrated she was with the way people took up more than one spot, and that she was going to park right in front of the building in the handicapped zone because everyone had wasted her time, and she had to visit someone.

I had enough of the negative for the morning. I told her I liked her CC hat (sort of like a Love Your Melon cap), and instantly, like a light switch, her demeanor changed to a lightened smile. I did mention that she should probably move her vehicle or it would get tagged and possibly towed. I was on my way out, so I am not sure what she decided.

It made me think of a recent Vikings/Eagles game and how fans were throwing expletives, cans, bottles, and other stuff at people and buses. At that moment, instead of saying, "I really like your jersey," to one of the offenders, I might have wanted to body slam someone for being rude and dangerous.

In reflection this morning, many of us have daily crises, and it wouldn't hurt to give out a sincere compliment to maybe change the mood, even if for a moment.

By the way, did I tell you that "you are something spectacular!"? If you don't feel that way now, I bet you can get there.

Need Some Socks

In the recent past, I was given the unexpected surprise at the Minnesota Veterans Home of witnessing a South Minneapolis man being honored posthumously in a dedication for serving in the Vietnam War.

For many of us, this was a misunderstood conflict, where our young men and women served our country, and as Americans we sat on both sides of the fence as to whether it was justified.

His family, news media, workers, and volunteers attended a ceremony for this man, Schmidt, honored prior with the Purple Heart and Silver Star for his bravery in serving us and protecting his fellow platoon mates in the Tet offensive.

He survived this ordeal, suffering from PTSD, and feeling some of the alienation when he came back home to US soil, and possibly not getting the attention he deserved.

One of his sisters told the story of how he would ask their mother to send him as many socks as possible, while in Southeast Asia. Many people wondered why he didn't ask for smokes, candy, something to read, or other amenities. He was insistent on socks.

They found out later, that he was giving pairs to his fellow platoon members because they wore out so frequently, to the point where he went "sockless," so his friends had some comfort in difficult times.

To me, this said much about this man, who succumbed to suicide a few years after he arrived home from a conflict we can only imagine.

This simple gesture gave others comfort, security, a sense that someone cared for them, and temporarily dry feet.

One Aspect of Ethical Leaders

One aspect of great ethical leaders is they know that the world is larger than what they want or desire. They also know there is a higher calling, where they take a stance for the greater good. Out of a sense of duty, they do what they believe is right, usually for the common good. Charisma and the ability to communicate influence the ability to lead, but somehow the true ethical leader has a definable quality to reach a group or the masses, to in turn feel compelled to do something for the greater good, and feel energized about it.

Generosity

There's a man I know who is famous for his apple pies, but more importantly, for his generosity. Each year, when all is said and done, he will make 63+ pies, and deliver them to colleagues and his neighbors, right before Thanksgiving. He is funny, altruistic, and often will answer a question with a verse from a song. One day I asked him how the "Pie Day" started.

He told me when he was a kid, they were dirt poor. His mom would sometimes serve a pie for dinner, but not for dessert. He mentioned that he wanted to be able to cook an entire Thanksgiving meal, so with a little instruction and encouragement from his mom, he became rather equipped to perform this task.

In 1992, maybe 1993, he started making pies that in his mom's estimation, were better than hers! "Don – Add a bit more salt. A little more cinnamon. Back off on the sugar." So, as the years went on, he made it a tradition, and brought in these famous apple pies that continue to delight the taste buds of recipients.

Please Be Careful

Here is a story told by Retired General Paul Kelley about one of his troops, John Banchini. It is a story about John's last words.

It was 1966, in Vietnam, during a battle intended to capture a cluster of hills. Kelley was a Colonel and John Banchini was his point man.

"Suddenly there was an explosion," recounted Kelley. "I saw John Banchini drop. John Banchini knew, knew, he was dying."

John Banchini said to Kelley, "Please be careful, Colonel. The hill is mined." His last words to Kelley were, "Please be careful, Colonel."

That's who General Kelley talks to when he visits the memorial.

"I go over to the memorial and I'll find John Banchini's name, and I'll put my hand on it, and I'll talk to John," he said.

In that moment, Banchini's only thoughts were to care for his leader with a warning. For some, this is incomprehensible, but Banchini had a heart.

On this celebrated Veteran's Day, maybe we could take that extra step to look out for people who need us.

Positivity

Someone recently expressed to me, "I wish I could be as positive as you. It seems like my life is just meant to be nothing but misery and pain, and truthfully, some days I just wish it all would end. No happiness, no purpose."

When someone says this or a variation of this narrative to me, I am not wired to just say, "Good luck, and I am sorry." Sometimes, it requires the person to get additional help. Sometimes, they need a nudge to see how they are an incredible gift to this world, yet they haven't realized it. Sometimes, no matter what is said or done, you cannot sway their heart and soul.

At this stage in my life as a teacher and man, I sometimes wish I could focus more on the content of what I was trained to do, continue to study and apply what I have learned from experience, and build people up by seeing their strengths and communicating to them what I have witnessed.

I originally went into this profession to inspire, motivate, and with the help of God and countless others who guided me, change lives for the good.

Often, I have seen someone turn the corner and see their own unique abilities and potential. Often, I have seen someone give an awe-inspiring speech that changed people's perspectives and made just about everyone in the room see that they too could make someone's day a little brighter and that their own inbred cynicism dial could turn toward seeing hope and possibilities for positive change.

I have seen young and old come up with innovative ways to handle mental illness, create business startups or an invention, figure out a new way to teach students to read, critique how we as educators can use more inclusive language, and also find ways to assist in making our own organizations more effective and ethical in what we do in daily business practice.

Life does have misery and pain. I too, have had my share. Happiness may come in small doses, and a small cup is all it may take to get you back to believing that there is joy, and the world does have very good people in it. We can provide that small cup to the recipe.

Yes. Some people are misguided. Some are not kind. Some have been egregiously wronged and are lashing out. Others just do not know that they are excellent, but they may need you to point it out.

We do have a responsibility to coach people within our scope of influence. Sometimes, it seems like too much effort. But at this time and place, we need all of us to not get too isolated and give up on humanity. There are people who truly need you.

How Do You Want to Spend Your Remaining Days?

In September, 2001, I was teaching sophomores in an early-morning class in high school. We had just turned our TV monitors on, having been told by our principal that one of the twin towers in NYC had been hit by a plane. Within minutes of the coverage, another one struck, and all of our lives changed in that unforgettable epoch in time, losing 3000+ friends, colleagues and fellow Americans, most of whom we had never met—but we all felt our diminishment and loss as a nation. And we hurt. I will never forget that day, the children entrusted to my care, and the ramifications it had for all of us.

So many first responders rallied to help, rescue, and mitigate the terror that suddenly hit us and sheared us at our core. As communities, as a country, the fate of our humanity was struggling in the balance.

I am still thankful for how we stepped up in those tragic days in our own communities, remaining sorry for lives lost, but continuing to remain hopeful about how we move forward.

I talked with a man yesterday who was complaining about so many aspects of his life that had gone wrong, were unfulfilling, and how life had treated him so unfairly.

At first, I listened somewhat inattentively. I was on my way to teach an evening class, having just scrambled to find parking.

I just happened to be in his path to the entrance door, and he seemed to need an ear.

You could see in his eyes and face the pain he had.

"Do you have some time for me?" I had fifty-five minutes before class but wasn't feeling fully present.

He continued to explain how life had become very difficult, to the point where he was almost numb from day-to-day life.

I shared that I too have those moments and question the meaning and purpose I have sometimes, especially when I am tired.

Setting some limits is important in our lives, and after listening some more, and then sharing a few of my own stories that might break him out of his funk, I finally said, "How many summers do you have left?"

He went silent. Continuing on, I said, "I mean...how do you want to spend the remaining good days of your life?"

Once again, I was reminded that we may not feel like we have the time to give, but in giving what we have in that moment—we can provide a small element of solace and care for someone who reaches out.

I will see this man again, and we will have coffee.

Remind Us of Our Value

Isolde Fair and an all young women's orchestra perform a powerful song about believing in yourself. Let your daughters and sons know that they have value. We can build a young person's confidence to make good choices and treat others with respect, dignity, and kindness.

See That Light

See that light? That is the sun rising. That is you. Each day you wake up, make the coffee, tea, or juice, start a new experience, seize the day, face some problems, laugh, cry, feel the joy, ride a wave, maybe swim against the current, and your sun sets for the day, and you rest. Then, you wake up the next day and emerge for another round. Capture that light you have and share it. That is you. Somewhere out there, someone needs what you have to offer.

Looking Out for One Another

How much more senseless killing and violence do we need to see, endure, watch, and helplessly witness before we as a society do something about it? I believe we have become unaffected by the loss of our own people.

El Paso and now Dayton are just two examples of this senseless violence and loss of life, and yet some of us can't even make a conscious effort to talk with our neighbors or family due to political rifts, losing control, or because of our differences. We are better than this. These past two events mark the 249th and 250th mass shootings this year alone.

An individual I spoke with recently admitted years later that she couldn't eat a "welcome to the neighborhood" hot dish for fear it could be tainted. An act of goodness is now considered suspicious, when it could be viewed as a way to connect.

In the United States, we came together connecting in 1776 to unite and form our own independent nation, one which many other countries still look to for direction and setting an example.

I am proud of our country, but are we losing sight of what we fought so hard to gain in freedom? With freedom comes responsibility—a responsibility to look out for one another.

Are we taking care of our brothers, sisters, and those in our midst, or are we becoming more secluded, fearful, and waiting for the next tragedy to occur?

My heart goes out to those who have suffered, are suffering, and to all of us who can make some positive difference in this world, which belongs to each one of us.

Small Manageable Steps

Life is unpredictable.

Someone inquired about pursuing a degree in leadership in our program. After a little discussion, we determined that the program was not for him at this time. I soon discovered that he needed someone to talk out some major issues he was facing in life.

In exasperation, he asked me, "Why should I even try? My efforts are never noticed or appreciated."

Maybe you have felt like you have been in this spot sometime in your life.

The person I was talking with added that he had just lost his job and had to sell his house. He also wanted to quit his existing position and find something more meaningful with better pay.

I acknowledged that these are difficult places to be, but encouraged him to focus on the manageable aspects, reflect on the goodness he had now, and tackle each problem with patience. Also, I reminded him that not everyone is going to appreciate your efforts, or let you know what you mean to them, but savor the times when someone gives you a compliment or sees your goodness.

Trying to go back to school, manage debt, find a new job, find a new place to live, deal with a pandemic like Covid-19, and support a family all at the same time is extremely stressful and hard on the heart.

In the grand scheme, after a lengthy discussion, he realized that he actually had it pretty good, but the stress of not having a job better suited to him was making everything else seem much worse.

Earlier in the day, I met with a mentor in my own life, who gave me some valuable reality checks. Once again, I have found that to be a good mentor, I also need good people to mentor me.

Later that day, I acknowledged to the person seeking guidance that I do not have all the answers, but the predicament will soon pass or resolve itself by creating a new chapter in his life.

By taking smaller more manageable steps to tackle one goal or issue at a time, life may actually get better and help you to see your new direction with more clarity.

Stuck in the Muck

You have no idea how much of a positive impact you can continue to be. At this point in my life, I cannot take a day for granted. Time is fleeting and escaping all of us as we speak.

When you are in your deepest trough of anguish or despair, what it is like to emerge from the muck? When you are in a hole, what do you do to climb out?

Some of us have a difficult time being in the hole, and we continue to stay there. If it is dark outside of the hole, you might want to cocoon down below for short periods or longer durations. But eventually, the sun is going to shine again. Yes. The sun is going to shine again.

Each of you in your own way have been friends, mentors, and advocates for life—to me. Some of you have known me personally for years. Others are connected exclusively in cyberspace. Gratitude to you.

What we all have in common is our humanity.

Moving one step at a time truly helps when you are stuck in the muck. When you are hungry, angry, lonely, or tired, you probably are not making your best decisions and can get stuck. (Notice that the first letter of each of these words spells HALT). Maybe stopping momentarily, or halting to ponder how you can take a few steps forward to meet your basic needs as a human being, can help. When we take care of some of these basic necessities to live our lives to the fullest, quite possibly, we eventually emerge from being stuck in the muck.

Taking Small Steps to Get Out of a Rut

One fall day, I hit a bad patch. I was in a rut. I was not sure if I was truly connecting, yet others say I do it very well. The funny thing is that what people perceive about you may not be the case in your own heart and soul. Sometimes life seems impossible.

Recently, someone sent me a long, detailed message describing a life ordeal they were going through. It was intensely painful to read, thoughtfully conveyed in words, and emotionally wrought with daily human suffering.

I threw my hands up in the air, speechless. I knew I couldn't solve it, take it on, pacify the situation, or completely offer the consolation and active listening ear this friend probably wanted. It seemed to me an impossible abyss to emerge from, with all the calamity and hurt they were experiencing.

Yet, I thought about how the "impossible" can take on a new meaning with the erasure of two letters: "im."

At the time, I was still in my own rut but slowly climbing out....

I'm not actually sure why. Maybe it is because I qualify for the 55+ senior menu in a few weeks? I should be grateful for discounts.

Maybe I am just insecure?

Maybe I question my own value? (Actually, I do, daily). Am I really making a difference?

Or maybe I should stop reflecting so much and just "do"?

Okay. Well... maybe when you keep moving, with your heart, soul, mind and of course your feet, you are making your day "possible." These are gifts that I often take for granted, and God, or if you prefer, a "higher power," gave you these for a reason.

You have a heart that pumps a staggering number of beats per day. A gift!

You have a soul that research and practice indicates cannot be fully duplicated. An incomprehensible gift!

You have a mind that has the capability to reason through myriad good and bad options each day. It is an astonishing gift with unlimited capacity!

And you have feet that give you the capability to walk forward or take baby steps toward meeting a challenge with courage. A gift not to be taken for granted!

I was in a rut. But I (and you) can make a change "possible." Maybe we need to take some small steps forward, especially when we get in a rut ourselves.

Tap on the Shoulder

Someone once stated that teachers are one of the "artists for developing people's human potential." As we start the new school year, I thank all of those individuals who guide others, whether it is our families, communities, mentors, coaches, or educators. What all of

PROFILES IN KINDNESS

you do does make a difference in a child's life. And the long-term effects are indelibly linked to that child's self-esteem, having them believe in themselves, and ultimately giving back to the next generation as an adult.

Often, the opportunity to help change someone's life for the better stares you right in the face. Other times, you may get that "tap on the shoulder," (as my friend Craig mentioned one day) to talk to someone who may truly need you to "pay attention."

We never truly know what someone is going through.

We have to sometimes choose where we can best have an impact.

But sometimes we do not get to choose. The situation at that very moment may require you to use the joyful spirit, love, and experience that was given to you.

The Kid and His Shoes

We had a fire at well-known hotel in downtown Minneapolis, displacing around 200 people who were homeless or in transition. It just so happened that it occurred during Christmas Day, and there was still work being done to contain the fire and get people back on their feet.

Nineteen hours after it started, the fire continued to burn Christmas night at a building that was a former hotel but now housed those who needed a place to stay.

They said the fire started on the second floor and quickly spread through the building. Flames could be seen shooting from the roof in the pre-dawn hours.

First responders brought three people to the hospital, and all were expected to recover. No one was killed in the fire.

At the time, more than 200 people, many of them children, were without a place to stay.

When local officials called on people in Minnesota to bring supplies—diapers, socks, mittens, blankets—for the displaced people, the response was immediate and overwhelming.

As one example, a woman named Terry, her husband, and

five-month-old daughter were given diapers, clothes, blankets, and gloves donated by generous strangers.

"This really made my day, this alone really made my day," she said.

In just a few hours, so many supply donations came in that officials had to stop accepting them. Instead, they asked people to give money.

In our Twin Cities community, many generous people went down to bring items, in many cases their own gifts received, to families who lost most if not all of their belongings in the fire.

Plenty of individuals have helped in this effort, and there are many stories of goodness.

I wanted to focus on just one that impacted me.

A young man alerted his parents that he wanted to give away his new t-shirt, and a toy he received this holiday. His mother was surprised and didn't want to curb his enthusiasm, so they planned to head downtown to give away his presents.

Mom noticed that her pre-teen son had also convinced his siblings to give away something, too. After a little cajoling, they realized the significance, and that it would be the right thing to do.

So Mom and her eldest son jumped in the car, gifts in the backseat. She noticed that he also had a pair of shoes on his lap.

Mom thought to herself, *No way!*

At a previous Timberwolves game, the New Jersey Nets were in town, and her son stood in line to have his shoes signed by the Phenom, Kyrie Irving. According to his mom, he loved those shoes, "eating, sleeping, and breathing in them" on a daily basis. They were still in excellent shape.

Mom's eyes started to well up with tears, sensing what her son planned to do.

She was conflicted and proud of her son, yet she also didn't want him to give up his prized possession.

"I am going to give these to someone who wears my size." He continued, "Kyrie inspired me. Maybe, I can inspire someone else."

I have hope for our future as a nation. There are plenty of young people who are servant leaders and see the impact they can make.

Unnecessary Noise

Life has a funny way of directing us where we need to be at the moment. A wise person once said to me, "You cannot control the uncontrollable. But you can turn down the unnecessary noise."

Walking with Someone Else's Difficulties

Back in the early '90s I was in the midst of a personal crisis. My marriage relationship was over. I had two young children, was trying to balance leaving an insurance career to make it as a teacher and be a "good" dad, which at times was a new discovery and challenge each day. I can say that I often just haphazardly learned a new parenting skill each day with my kids, adapting as the situation warranted.

Making a career switch was a little daunting for me. I had a BA degree but found out quickly that if I wanted to be an educator, I needed a master's, licensure for K-12, and licensure for teaching at a technical college. Eventually, to do a study to help others figure out their best way of acquiring information and trying to understand learning styles, I pursued a doctorate, many times bringing my daughters with me to the U of M to finish my research.

After getting a master's, to make this career change work, I took a risk. I taught concurrently at four different places, and sometimes I would put my head in my hands and question my decision to go the education route. My daughters were very patient with their dad. We would play games, sometimes go to the mall for rides, listen to music of many varieties and sing along, have picnics, and laugh. Then, I would put them back in their car seats, arrive at our destination at the St. Paul campus, unbuckle them, get them a snack, bring some books, laugh and play again, holding one daughter's hand, while holding my other baby munchkin in the other. Somehow, I carried my bag of books, too.

Moms and dads do this every day. I am not complaining, but I do

LEADERSHIP

know that this period was trying. I made it through, like most of us do.

I think back to this time and am very indebted to those who did not let me fail. Many times, I did falter and stumble. But somehow, someone would magically appear to rescue me from giving up.

Maybe like you, when you feel overwhelmed, you feel alone and that no one cares for you, especially when you are tired and stressed.

When you feel alone, you have to face yourself and feel what you are made of. For many like me, this is still difficult.

Once again, I am fortunate that you were there for me. I could mention names. But you know who you are.

It is said that you truly respect someone when they walk with you in your difficulties. They don't just respect you. They love you.

Batter's Box

One of our vets was ribbing me about missing a few pitches.

"I bet you take many swings and whiff often."

I thought for a few seconds, and said, "I do take many swings, and occasionally I miss. But you can't hit the ball if you don't step into the batter's box."

Last Advice

1. Life isn't fair, but it's still good.
2. When in doubt, just take the next small step.
3. Life is too short to waste time hating anyone.
4. Your job won't take care of you when you are sick. Your friends and parents will. Stay in touch.
5. Pay off your credit cards every month.
6. You don't have to win every argument. Agree to disagree.
7. Cry with someone. It's more healing than crying alone.
8. It's okay to get angry with God. God can take it.
9. Save for retirement, starting with your first paycheck.
10. When it comes to chocolate, resistance is futile.
11. Make peace with your past so it won't screw up the present.
12. It's okay to let your children see you cry.

13. Don't compare your life to others' lives. You have no idea what their journey is all about.
14. If a relationship has to be a secret, you shouldn't be in it.
15. Everything can change in the blink of an eye.
16. Take a deep breath. It calms the mind.
17. Get rid of anything that isn't useful, beautiful, or joyful.
18. Whatever doesn't kill you really does make you stronger.
19. It's never too late to have a happy childhood. But the second one is up to you and no one else.
20. When it comes to going after what you love in life, don't take no for an answer.
21. Over prepare. Then go with the flow.
22. Be eccentric now. Be unique.
23. The most important organs you have are your brain and your heart.
24. No one is in charge of your happiness but you.
25. Frame every so-called disaster with these words: "In five years, will this matter?"
26. Always choose life.
27. Forgive everyone everything.
28. What other people think of you is none of your business.
29. Time heals almost everything. Give time time.
30. Not everyone is going to like you.
31. However good or bad a situation is, it will change.
32. Don't take yourself so seriously. No one else does.
33. Believe in miracles.
34. God loves you because of who God is, not because of anything you did or didn't do.
35. Don't audit life. Show up and make the most of it now.
36. Growing old beats the alternative—dying young.
37. Your children get only one childhood.
38. All that truly matters in the end is that you loved.
39. It was said in the beginning of this book: "Get outside every day. Miracles are waiting everywhere."

LEADERSHIP

40. If we all threw our problems in a pile and saw everyone else's, we'd grab ours back.
41. Envy is a waste of time. You already have all you need.
42. The best is yet to come....
43. No matter how you feel, get up, dress up, and show up.
44. Yield.
45. Life isn't tied with a bow, but it's still a gift.

About the Author

Dr. Kotz has written two other books: The CIPA Award winning *Something Happened Today* (2018), which discusses stories of mentorship, as well as keeping your eyes and ears open to the present and the positive. It addresses seeing the good each day, facing difficulties and adversity with hope and compassion. Also, *Personality, Gender and Learning Styles – Teaching to Student Aptitudes* (2014), investigates our preferred learning and personality styles and how they affect our ability to acquire new information.

Kotz currently teaches the subjects of Ethics, Organizational Effectiveness, Strategies for Adult Learning Theory, and Statistical Research Methods at Saint Mary's University of Minnesota - Doctorate in Leadership program. He brings practical decision tools and discussion to assisting in creating present-day opportunities and dealing with difficult situations that we all face in our organizations. Prior to his teaching career, he was a reinsurance actuary in both life and property casualty insurance. He also served as a manager for customer service at North American Life and Casualty prior to his education pursuits and served as director for General Education at Anoka Hennepin Technical College.

Some of his articles published and presentations include: *Teaching Examples of Extraordinary Leadership – Influence and Inspiration – An Ethnographic Study*; *Women Who Have Run for President - An Examination of Leadership Qualities* (2016; 2018); *Reaching Millennials in the Classroom* (2013). In addition, he continues to give motivational talks on examples of influence and inspiration, seeing the unique gifts that we all possess.

Dr. Kotz is a lifelong learner with education and business expertise. This includes working as faculty and advisor with undergraduate and graduate students. Kotz has taught and served as an executive/life coach to graduate students and business professionals and has assisted high school students in navigating adolescence. He is a resident of Saint Paul, Minnesota and continues to collect new experiences that shape and challenge his perspectives.

Please feel free to write him at pkotz@smumn.edu or paulekotz@yahoo.com

Also by
PAUL E. KOTZ

Something Happened Today

There are times in my life, when I wasn't truly looking around to see the goodness that exists. I am extremely lucky to have people who have mentored me along the way by their examples, words and actions to look for the good. I have learned and witnessed that if you open your eyes and ears, you can live your life staying present to the positive. This book is just that. It is a collection of stories that may inspire you, challenge you, or let you see a situation in an entirely new way.

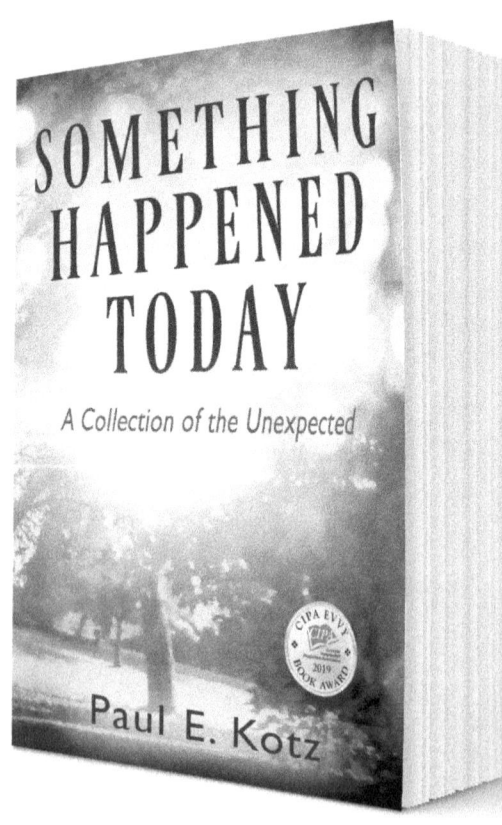

Learn more at:
www.outskirtspress.com/somethinghappenedtoday

CPSIA information can be obtained
at www.ICGtesting.com
Printed in the USA
FSHW010232230420
69440FS

9 781977 224330